50 30-Minute Weeknight Recipes for Home

By: Kelly Johnson

Table of Contents

- Spaghetti Aglio e Olio
- Sheet Pan Lemon Herb Chicken with Vegetables
- Beef Stir-Fry with Bell Peppers and Broccoli
- Vegetarian Chickpea Curry
- One-Pot Creamy Tomato Basil Pasta
- Honey Garlic Shrimp Stir-Fry
- Teriyaki Tofu with Vegetables
- Lemon Butter Chicken with Asparagus
- Cauliflower Fried Rice
- BBQ Chicken Quesadillas
- Creamy Mushroom and Spinach Tortellini
- Garlic Butter Salmon with Roasted Vegetables
- Greek Chicken Gyros with Tzatziki Sauce
- Thai Basil Beef Stir-Fry
- Caprese Stuffed Chicken Breast
- Vegetarian Black Bean Enchiladas
- Lemon Garlic Butter Shrimp with Zucchini Noodles
- One-Pot Chicken Alfredo Pasta
- Quinoa and Black Bean Stuffed Bell Peppers
- Sheet Pan Fajitas (Chicken or Beef)
- Creamy Parmesan Garlic Mushroom Chicken
- Spicy Peanut Noodles with Vegetables
- Baked Teriyaki Salmon with Broccoli
- Veggie-Packed Turkey Meatballs with Marinara Sauce
- Lemon Herb Grilled Chicken with Quinoa
- Creamy Tuscan Garlic Chicken
- Black Bean and Corn Quesadillas
- Honey Sriracha Chicken with Rice
- Spinach and Ricotta Stuffed Shells
- Moroccan Chickpea Stew
- Garlic Butter Steak Bites with Potatoes
- Vegetable Stir-Fry with Tofu
- One-Pot Cajun Pasta
- Baked Lemon Herb Cod with Green Beans
- Creamy Pesto Pasta with Cherry Tomatoes

- Teriyaki Veggie Stir-Fry
- Italian Sausage and Peppers with Polenta
- Shrimp Scampi with Linguine
- Veggie-Packed Turkey Chili
- Lemon Garlic Butter Shrimp and Asparagus
- Vegetarian Pad Thai
- Creamy Mushroom Spinach Tortellini Soup
- Sheet Pan Garlic Herb Pork Chops with Potatoes
- Baked Honey Mustard Chicken with Brussels Sprouts
- Coconut Curry Shrimp with Rice
- Veggie Quesadillas with Guacamole
- One-Pot Lemon Herb Chicken and Rice
- Black Bean and Corn Stuffed Sweet Potatoes
- Creamy Tomato Basil Soup with Grilled Cheese
- Szechuan Tofu and Green Beans Stir-Fry

Spaghetti Aglio e Olio

Ingredients:

- 8 ounces (225g) spaghetti
- 4 cloves garlic, thinly sliced
- 1/4 cup (60ml) extra virgin olive oil
- 1/2 teaspoon red pepper flakes (adjust to taste)
- Salt, to taste
- Freshly ground black pepper, to taste
- 2 tablespoons chopped fresh parsley
- Grated Parmesan cheese, for serving (optional)

Instructions:

1. Cook the spaghetti according to package instructions in a large pot of salted boiling water until al dente. Reserve about 1/2 cup of pasta cooking water, then drain the spaghetti and set aside.
2. While the spaghetti is cooking, heat the olive oil in a large skillet over medium heat. Add the sliced garlic and red pepper flakes. Cook, stirring frequently, until the garlic is golden brown and fragrant, about 2-3 minutes. Be careful not to burn the garlic.
3. Add the cooked spaghetti to the skillet with the garlic and oil. Toss well to coat the spaghetti evenly with the garlic-infused oil. If the pasta seems dry, add some of the reserved pasta cooking water, a little at a time, until you reach your desired consistency.
4. Season the spaghetti with salt and black pepper to taste. Stir in the chopped parsley and toss again to combine.
5. Serve the spaghetti aglio e olio immediately, garnished with grated Parmesan cheese if desired. Enjoy!

This dish is perfect for a quick and satisfying weeknight meal.

Sheet Pan Lemon Herb Chicken with Vegetables

Ingredients:

- 4 boneless, skinless chicken breasts
- 1 pound (450g) baby potatoes, halved
- 2 cups (300g) baby carrots
- 1 red bell pepper, sliced
- 1 yellow bell pepper, sliced
- 1/4 cup (60ml) olive oil
- 3 cloves garlic, minced
- 2 tablespoons fresh lemon juice
- 1 teaspoon lemon zest
- 1 tablespoon chopped fresh parsley
- 1 tablespoon chopped fresh thyme
- Salt, to taste
- Black pepper, to taste
- Lemon slices, for garnish (optional)

Instructions:

1. Preheat your oven to 400°F (200°C). Line a large baking sheet with parchment paper or aluminum foil for easy cleanup.
2. In a small bowl, whisk together the olive oil, minced garlic, lemon juice, lemon zest, chopped parsley, chopped thyme, salt, and black pepper.
3. Place the chicken breasts in a large resealable plastic bag or shallow dish. Pour half of the lemon herb marinade over the chicken, making sure it's evenly coated. Reserve the remaining marinade for the vegetables.
4. In a separate bowl, toss the halved baby potatoes, baby carrots, and sliced bell peppers with the remaining marinade until well coated.
5. Arrange the marinated chicken breasts in the center of the prepared baking sheet. Spread the marinated vegetables around the chicken in a single layer.
6. Bake in the preheated oven for 20-25 minutes, or until the chicken is cooked through (internal temperature reaches 165°F/75°C) and the vegetables are tender, stirring the vegetables halfway through cooking.
7. Once done, remove the sheet pan from the oven. Allow the chicken to rest for a few minutes before slicing.

8. Serve the lemon herb chicken alongside the roasted vegetables on a serving platter. Garnish with lemon slices and additional chopped herbs if desired. Enjoy your delicious and wholesome meal!

This Sheet Pan Lemon Herb Chicken with Vegetables is not only flavorful but also a convenient option for a satisfying weeknight dinner.

Beef Stir-Fry with Bell Peppers and Broccoli

Ingredients:

- 1 lb (450g) beef sirloin, thinly sliced against the grain
- 2 tablespoons soy sauce
- 1 tablespoon oyster sauce
- 1 tablespoon hoisin sauce
- 2 teaspoons cornstarch
- 1 tablespoon vegetable oil
- 3 cloves garlic, minced
- 1 teaspoon minced ginger
- 1 red bell pepper, sliced
- 1 green bell pepper, sliced
- 2 cups broccoli florets
- Salt and pepper, to taste
- Cooked rice or noodles, for serving
- Sesame seeds and sliced green onions, for garnish (optional)

Instructions:

1. In a bowl, combine the soy sauce, oyster sauce, hoisin sauce, and cornstarch. Add the sliced beef to the bowl and toss until evenly coated. Let it marinate for about 15-20 minutes.
2. Heat the vegetable oil in a large skillet or wok over medium-high heat. Add the minced garlic and ginger, and sauté for about 30 seconds until fragrant.
3. Add the marinated beef to the skillet in a single layer. Cook for 2-3 minutes, stirring occasionally, until the beef is browned but still slightly pink in the center. Remove the beef from the skillet and set it aside.
4. In the same skillet, add a little more oil if needed. Add the sliced bell peppers and broccoli florets. Stir-fry for 3-4 minutes until the vegetables are crisp-tender.
5. Return the cooked beef to the skillet with the vegetables. Stir everything together and cook for an additional 1-2 minutes to heat through.
6. Season the stir-fry with salt and pepper to taste. If desired, you can add a splash of soy sauce or oyster sauce for extra flavor.

7. Serve the beef stir-fry with bell peppers and broccoli over cooked rice or noodles. Garnish with sesame seeds and sliced green onions if desired. Enjoy your delicious and nutritious meal!

This beef stir-fry is not only tasty and satisfying but also a great way to incorporate plenty of veggies into your meal.

Vegetarian Chickpea Curry

Ingredients:

- 2 tablespoons vegetable oil
- 1 onion, diced
- 3 cloves garlic, minced
- 1 tablespoon minced ginger
- 1 tablespoon curry powder
- 1 teaspoon ground cumin
- 1 teaspoon ground coriander
- 1/2 teaspoon turmeric
- 1/4 teaspoon cayenne pepper (optional, for heat)
- 1 can (15 ounces/425g) chickpeas, drained and rinsed
- 1 can (14 ounces/400ml) diced tomatoes
- 1 can (13.5 ounces/400ml) coconut milk
- 2 cups (240g) baby spinach leaves
- Salt and pepper, to taste
- Fresh cilantro, chopped, for garnish
- Cooked rice or naan bread, for serving

Instructions:

1. Heat the vegetable oil in a large skillet or saucepan over medium heat. Add the diced onion and cook for 5-6 minutes until softened and translucent.
2. Add the minced garlic and ginger to the skillet and cook for an additional 1-2 minutes until fragrant.
3. Stir in the curry powder, ground cumin, ground coriander, turmeric, and cayenne pepper (if using). Cook for 1 minute until the spices are toasted and fragrant.
4. Add the drained chickpeas to the skillet and stir to coat them in the spice mixture.
5. Pour in the diced tomatoes (with their juices) and coconut milk. Stir well to combine all the ingredients.
6. Bring the curry to a simmer and let it cook for 10-15 minutes, stirring occasionally, until the sauce has thickened slightly and the flavors have melded together.

7. Stir in the baby spinach leaves and cook for an additional 2-3 minutes until wilted.
8. Season the chickpea curry with salt and pepper to taste.
9. Serve the vegetarian chickpea curry hot over cooked rice or with naan bread. Garnish with fresh chopped cilantro before serving. Enjoy your flavorful and nutritious meal!

This vegetarian chickpea curry is not only delicious and satisfying but also easy to customize with your favorite vegetables and spices.

One-Pot Creamy Tomato Basil Pasta

Ingredients:

- 8 ounces (225g) dried pasta (such as penne or spaghetti)
- 1 tablespoon olive oil
- 3 cloves garlic, minced
- 1 can (14 ounces/400g) diced tomatoes
- 2 cups (480ml) vegetable broth
- 1/2 cup (120ml) heavy cream or coconut cream for a vegan option
- 1/4 cup (60ml) tomato paste
- 1 teaspoon dried basil (or 2 tablespoons chopped fresh basil)
- 1/2 teaspoon dried oregano
- Salt and pepper, to taste
- Grated Parmesan cheese, for serving (optional)
- Fresh basil leaves, torn, for garnish

Instructions:

1. In a large pot or Dutch oven, heat the olive oil over medium heat. Add the minced garlic and cook for 1-2 minutes until fragrant.
2. Add the dried pasta to the pot, along with the diced tomatoes (with their juices), vegetable broth, heavy cream, tomato paste, dried basil, dried oregano, salt, and pepper. Stir well to combine all the ingredients.
3. Bring the mixture to a boil, then reduce the heat to medium-low. Cover the pot and simmer for about 15-20 minutes, stirring occasionally, until the pasta is cooked al dente and the sauce has thickened.
4. Once the pasta is cooked, taste and adjust the seasoning as needed with more salt and pepper.
5. If desired, sprinkle grated Parmesan cheese over the creamy tomato basil pasta before serving.
6. Serve the pasta hot, garnished with torn fresh basil leaves for extra flavor and freshness. Enjoy your creamy and comforting one-pot meal!

This one-pot creamy tomato basil pasta is a quick and easy dish that's sure to become a family favorite. Plus, it's all made in just one pot, which means fewer dishes to wash!

Honey Garlic Shrimp Stir-Fry

Ingredients:

- 1 lb (450g) shrimp, peeled and deveined
- 2 tablespoons soy sauce
- 2 tablespoons honey
- 3 cloves garlic, minced
- 1 tablespoon grated ginger
- 1 tablespoon sesame oil
- 1 tablespoon vegetable oil
- 1 bell pepper, thinly sliced
- 1 cup (150g) sugar snap peas or snow peas
- 2 green onions, sliced
- Cooked rice or noodles, for serving
- Sesame seeds, for garnish (optional)
- Sliced green onions, for garnish (optional)

Instructions:

1. In a small bowl, whisk together the soy sauce, honey, minced garlic, and grated ginger to make the sauce.
2. Heat the vegetable oil and sesame oil in a large skillet or wok over medium-high heat.
3. Add the shrimp to the skillet in a single layer. Cook for 1-2 minutes on each side until they turn pink and opaque. Remove the cooked shrimp from the skillet and set aside.
4. In the same skillet, add the sliced bell pepper and sugar snap peas. Stir-fry for 2-3 minutes until the vegetables are crisp-tender.
5. Return the cooked shrimp to the skillet with the vegetables. Pour the honey garlic sauce over the shrimp and vegetables.
6. Stir-fry everything together for an additional 1-2 minutes until the shrimp are coated in the sauce and everything is heated through.
7. Taste and adjust the seasoning if needed. You can add more soy sauce or honey according to your taste preferences.

8. Serve the honey garlic shrimp stir-fry hot over cooked rice or noodles. Garnish with sesame seeds and sliced green onions if desired. Enjoy your delicious and flavorful meal!

This honey garlic shrimp stir-fry is quick, easy, and packed with flavor. It's sure to become a favorite in your weeknight dinner rotation!

Teriyaki Tofu with Vegetables

Ingredients:

- 1 block (14-16 ounces/400-450g) firm tofu, pressed and cubed
- 2 tablespoons cornstarch
- 2 tablespoons soy sauce
- 2 tablespoons rice vinegar
- 2 tablespoons mirin (Japanese sweet rice wine)
- 2 tablespoons honey or maple syrup for a vegan option
- 1 tablespoon sesame oil
- 3 cloves garlic, minced
- 1 tablespoon minced ginger
- 1 cup (150g) broccoli florets
- 1 bell pepper, sliced
- 1 carrot, julienned or sliced into matchsticks
- 1/2 cup (120ml) teriyaki sauce (store-bought or homemade)
- Cooked rice, for serving
- Sesame seeds and sliced green onions, for garnish (optional)

Instructions:

1. Start by pressing the tofu to remove excess moisture. Place the tofu block between two layers of paper towels or clean kitchen towels. Place a heavy object, like a skillet or a few cans, on top of the tofu and let it sit for about 15-20 minutes. Then, cut the tofu into cubes.
2. In a shallow bowl, toss the tofu cubes with cornstarch until they are evenly coated.
3. In a small bowl, whisk together the soy sauce, rice vinegar, mirin, and honey (or maple syrup) to make the teriyaki sauce. Set aside.
4. Heat the sesame oil in a large skillet or wok over medium-high heat. Add the minced garlic and ginger, and cook for about 1 minute until fragrant.
5. Add the tofu cubes to the skillet in a single layer. Cook for 3-4 minutes on each side until they are golden brown and crispy. Remove the tofu from the skillet and set aside.

6. In the same skillet, add a little more sesame oil if needed. Add the broccoli florets, sliced bell pepper, and julienned carrot. Stir-fry for about 3-4 minutes until the vegetables are crisp-tender.
7. Return the cooked tofu to the skillet with the vegetables. Pour the teriyaki sauce over the tofu and vegetables.
8. Stir everything together and cook for an additional 1-2 minutes until the sauce thickens slightly and coats the tofu and vegetables.
9. Serve the teriyaki tofu with vegetables hot over cooked rice. Garnish with sesame seeds and sliced green onions if desired. Enjoy your delicious and flavorful meal!

This teriyaki tofu with vegetables is a tasty and nutritious dish that's sure to satisfy vegetarians and non-vegetarians alike. It's packed with protein, vitamins, and minerals, making it a wholesome meal option for any day of the week!

Lemon Butter Chicken with Asparagus

Ingredients:

- 4 boneless, skinless chicken breasts
- Salt and black pepper, to taste
- 2 tablespoons olive oil
- 4 tablespoons unsalted butter
- 4 cloves garlic, minced
- Zest of 1 lemon
- Juice of 1 lemon
- 1 teaspoon dried thyme (or 1 tablespoon fresh thyme leaves)
- 1 bunch asparagus, woody ends trimmed
- Lemon slices, for garnish
- Chopped fresh parsley, for garnish

Instructions:

1. Season the chicken breasts on both sides with salt and black pepper according to your taste preferences.
2. Heat the olive oil in a large skillet over medium-high heat. Once the skillet is hot, add the chicken breasts and cook for 5-6 minutes on each side until they are golden brown and cooked through. Remove the chicken from the skillet and set it aside.
3. In the same skillet, reduce the heat to medium. Add the unsalted butter and minced garlic. Cook for 1-2 minutes until the garlic is fragrant and slightly golden.
4. Stir in the lemon zest, lemon juice, and dried thyme. Cook for another minute to allow the flavors to meld together.
5. Return the cooked chicken breasts to the skillet, turning them in the lemon butter sauce to coat them evenly. Cook for an additional 2-3 minutes, spooning the sauce over the chicken occasionally.
6. While the chicken is finishing cooking, add the trimmed asparagus spears to the skillet. Cook for 3-4 minutes, or until the asparagus is tender yet still crisp.
7. Once the chicken is fully cooked and the asparagus is tender, remove the skillet from the heat.
8. Serve the lemon butter chicken with asparagus hot, garnished with lemon slices and chopped fresh parsley. Enjoy your flavorful and vibrant meal!

This lemon butter chicken with asparagus is a light and refreshing dish that's bursting with citrusy flavors. It's perfect for a quick and elegant dinner any night of the week!

Cauliflower Fried Rice

Ingredients:

- 1 medium head of cauliflower
- 2 tablespoons vegetable oil or sesame oil
- 2 cloves garlic, minced
- 1 small onion, finely chopped
- 1 carrot, diced
- 1/2 cup frozen peas
- 2 eggs, beaten
- 3 tablespoons soy sauce (or tamari for a gluten-free option)
- 1 tablespoon oyster sauce (optional)
- Salt and pepper, to taste
- Chopped green onions, for garnish
- Sesame seeds, for garnish

Instructions:

1. Remove the leaves and core from the cauliflower and chop it into florets. Place the cauliflower florets in a food processor and pulse until they resemble rice grains. Alternatively, you can grate the cauliflower using a box grater.
2. Heat 1 tablespoon of vegetable oil or sesame oil in a large skillet or wok over medium-high heat. Add the minced garlic and chopped onion, and cook for 1-2 minutes until softened and fragrant.
3. Add the diced carrot and frozen peas to the skillet. Stir-fry for 2-3 minutes until the vegetables are tender-crisp.
4. Push the vegetables to one side of the skillet and add the beaten eggs to the empty side. Scramble the eggs until they are cooked through, then mix them with the vegetables.
5. Push the vegetable and egg mixture to the side again, and add the remaining tablespoon of oil to the empty side of the skillet. Add the riced cauliflower to the skillet.
6. Stir-fry the cauliflower for 4-5 minutes, stirring occasionally, until it is tender but not mushy.
7. Stir in the soy sauce and oyster sauce (if using), and season with salt and pepper to taste. Cook for an additional 1-2 minutes to allow the flavors to meld together.

8. Remove the skillet from the heat and garnish the cauliflower fried rice with chopped green onions and sesame seeds.
9. Serve the cauliflower fried rice hot as a delicious and healthy side dish or as a main course. Enjoy your flavorful and nutritious meal!

Cauliflower fried rice is a low-carb, gluten-free, and vegetable-packed alternative to traditional fried rice. It's quick and easy to make, making it perfect for a weeknight dinner or meal prep.

BBQ Chicken Quesadillas

Ingredients:

- 2 cups cooked shredded chicken (you can use rotisserie chicken or leftover cooked chicken)
- 1/2 cup barbecue sauce (use your favorite store-bought or homemade sauce)
- 4 large flour tortillas
- 2 cups shredded cheese (cheddar, Monterey Jack, or a blend)
- 1/2 red onion, thinly sliced (optional)
- 1/4 cup chopped fresh cilantro (optional)
- Vegetable oil, for cooking
- Sour cream, guacamole, and salsa, for serving (optional)

Instructions:

1. In a mixing bowl, combine the cooked shredded chicken with the barbecue sauce, tossing until the chicken is evenly coated.
2. Heat a large skillet or griddle over medium heat. Brush one side of a flour tortilla with a little vegetable oil.
3. Place the oiled side of the tortilla down onto the skillet. Spoon some of the barbecue chicken mixture evenly over half of the tortilla.
4. Sprinkle shredded cheese over the chicken, and add a few slices of red onion and chopped cilantro if desired.
5. Fold the empty half of the tortilla over the filling, creating a half-moon shape.
6. Cook the quesadilla for 2-3 minutes on each side, until golden brown and crispy, and the cheese is melted.
7. Remove the cooked quesadilla from the skillet and transfer it to a cutting board. Let it cool for a minute before slicing it into wedges.
8. Repeat the process with the remaining tortillas and filling ingredients.
9. Serve the BBQ chicken quesadillas hot with sour cream, guacamole, and salsa on the side for dipping, if desired.
10. Enjoy your delicious and flavorful BBQ chicken quesadillas as a quick and easy meal!

These quesadillas are customizable, so feel free to add any extra toppings you like, such as diced tomatoes, sliced jalapeños, or chopped avocado. They're perfect for a family dinner or a casual gathering with friends.

Creamy Mushroom and Spinach Tortellini

Ingredients:

- 1 lb (450g) cheese tortellini (fresh or frozen)
- 2 tablespoons butter
- 8 ounces (225g) cremini mushrooms, sliced
- 3 cloves garlic, minced
- 1 teaspoon dried thyme
- 1 teaspoon dried oregano
- 1/2 cup (120ml) vegetable broth or chicken broth
- 1 cup (240ml) heavy cream
- 2 cups (60g) baby spinach leaves
- 1/2 cup (50g) grated Parmesan cheese
- Salt and pepper, to taste
- Chopped fresh parsley, for garnish (optional)

Instructions:

1. Cook the tortellini according to the package instructions in a large pot of salted boiling water. Drain and set aside.
2. In a large skillet, melt the butter over medium heat. Add the sliced mushrooms and cook for 5-6 minutes until they are golden brown and tender.
3. Add the minced garlic, dried thyme, and dried oregano to the skillet. Cook for an additional 1-2 minutes until the garlic is fragrant.
4. Pour the vegetable broth into the skillet and deglaze the pan, scraping up any browned bits from the bottom. Let the broth simmer for 2-3 minutes until it reduces slightly.
5. Reduce the heat to low and stir in the heavy cream. Let the sauce simmer gently for 5-6 minutes until it thickens slightly.
6. Add the cooked tortellini to the skillet along with the baby spinach leaves. Stir everything together until the spinach wilts and the tortellini is coated in the creamy sauce.
7. Stir in the grated Parmesan cheese until it melts into the sauce. Season with salt and pepper to taste.
8. Remove the skillet from the heat and garnish the creamy mushroom and spinach tortellini with chopped fresh parsley, if desired.

9. Serve the tortellini hot, garnished with additional grated Parmesan cheese if desired. Enjoy your creamy and comforting meal!

This creamy mushroom and spinach tortellini is a satisfying and flavorful dish that's sure to become a family favorite. It's quick and easy to make, making it perfect for busy weeknights or lazy weekends.

Garlic Butter Salmon with Roasted Vegetables

Ingredients:

- 4 salmon fillets (about 6 ounces/170g each), skin-on or skinless
- Salt and black pepper, to taste
- 4 tablespoons unsalted butter, melted
- 4 cloves garlic, minced
- 1 tablespoon lemon juice
- 1 teaspoon lemon zest
- 1 teaspoon chopped fresh parsley (plus more for garnish)
- 1 pound (450g) mixed vegetables (such as broccoli, bell peppers, zucchini, and carrots), cut into bite-sized pieces
- 2 tablespoons olive oil
- Salt and black pepper, to taste
- Lemon wedges, for serving

Instructions:

1. Preheat your oven to 400°F (200°C). Line a baking sheet with parchment paper or aluminum foil for easy cleanup.
2. Place the salmon fillets on the prepared baking sheet, skin-side down if they have skin. Season the salmon with salt and black pepper to taste.
3. In a small bowl, mix together the melted butter, minced garlic, lemon juice, lemon zest, and chopped parsley. Spoon the garlic butter mixture evenly over the salmon fillets.
4. In a separate bowl, toss the mixed vegetables with olive oil until they are evenly coated. Season the vegetables with salt and black pepper to taste.
5. Arrange the seasoned vegetables around the salmon on the baking sheet in a single layer.
6. Roast the salmon and vegetables in the preheated oven for 12-15 minutes, or until the salmon is cooked through and flakes easily with a fork, and the vegetables are tender and slightly caramelized.
7. Once done, remove the baking sheet from the oven. Garnish the garlic butter salmon with additional chopped parsley and serve hot with lemon wedges on the side.
8. Enjoy your flavorful and nutritious garlic butter salmon with roasted vegetables!

This dish is not only delicious and easy to make but also packed with healthy omega-3 fatty acids from the salmon and an assortment of vitamins and minerals from the roasted vegetables. It's perfect for a wholesome weeknight dinner or a special occasion meal.

Greek Chicken Gyros with Tzatziki Sauce

Ingredients:

For the Greek Chicken:

- 1 lb (450g) boneless, skinless chicken breasts or thighs, thinly sliced
- 2 tablespoons olive oil
- 3 cloves garlic, minced
- 1 teaspoon dried oregano
- 1 teaspoon dried thyme
- 1 teaspoon paprika
- 1/2 teaspoon ground cumin
- Salt and pepper, to taste
- Juice of 1 lemon

For the Tzatziki Sauce:

- 1 cup (240g) Greek yogurt
- 1/2 cucumber, grated and squeezed to remove excess moisture
- 2 cloves garlic, minced
- 1 tablespoon lemon juice
- 1 tablespoon chopped fresh dill (or 1 teaspoon dried dill)
- Salt and pepper, to taste

For Serving:

- Pita bread or flatbread
- Sliced tomatoes
- Sliced red onion
- Sliced cucumbers
- Crumbled feta cheese
- Chopped fresh parsley, for garnish

Instructions:

1. In a bowl, combine the olive oil, minced garlic, dried oregano, dried thyme, paprika, ground cumin, salt, pepper, and lemon juice. Mix well to make the marinade.
2. Add the sliced chicken to the marinade and toss until the chicken is evenly coated. Cover the bowl and marinate the chicken in the refrigerator for at least 30 minutes, or up to 4 hours for best flavor.
3. While the chicken is marinating, prepare the tzatziki sauce. In a bowl, combine the Greek yogurt, grated cucumber, minced garlic, lemon juice, chopped fresh dill, salt, and pepper. Mix well to combine. Cover and refrigerate until ready to serve.
4. Preheat a grill or grill pan over medium-high heat. Remove the chicken from the marinade and thread it onto skewers if using. Discard any excess marinade.
5. Grill the chicken skewers for 4-5 minutes on each side, or until cooked through and lightly charred. Alternatively, you can cook the chicken in a skillet over medium-high heat for about 6-8 minutes, stirring occasionally, until cooked through.
6. Once the chicken is cooked, remove it from the grill or skillet and let it rest for a few minutes.
7. To assemble the gyros, warm the pita bread or flatbread in the oven or on the grill. Spread a generous amount of tzatziki sauce on each piece of bread.
8. Top the tzatziki sauce with the grilled chicken, sliced tomatoes, sliced red onion, sliced cucumbers, crumbled feta cheese, and chopped fresh parsley.
9. Fold the pita bread or flatbread over the filling to form a gyro. Serve immediately and enjoy your delicious Greek chicken gyros with tzatziki sauce!

These Greek chicken gyros are perfect for a casual meal or a gathering with friends and family. They're flavorful, satisfying, and sure to be a hit!

Thai Basil Beef Stir-Fry

Ingredients:

For the Beef Marinade:

- 1 lb (450g) beef steak (such as flank steak or sirloin), thinly sliced against the grain
- 2 tablespoons soy sauce
- 1 tablespoon oyster sauce
- 1 tablespoon fish sauce
- 1 teaspoon brown sugar
- 2 cloves garlic, minced
- 1 teaspoon grated ginger
- 1 teaspoon cornstarch

For the Stir-Fry:

- 2 tablespoons vegetable oil
- 4 cloves garlic, minced
- 1-2 red chili peppers, thinly sliced (adjust to taste)
- 1 bell pepper, thinly sliced
- 1 onion, thinly sliced
- 1 cup (30g) Thai basil leaves, loosely packed
- Cooked rice, for serving

Instructions:

1. In a bowl, combine the thinly sliced beef with soy sauce, oyster sauce, fish sauce, brown sugar, minced garlic, grated ginger, and cornstarch. Mix well to coat the beef evenly. Let it marinate for at least 15-20 minutes.
2. Heat vegetable oil in a large skillet or wok over high heat. Once hot, add the minced garlic and sliced chili peppers. Stir-fry for about 30 seconds until fragrant.
3. Add the marinated beef to the skillet in a single layer. Cook for 2-3 minutes without stirring to allow the beef to sear and develop a nice crust.

4. Stir-fry the beef for an additional 2-3 minutes until it is cooked through and evenly browned. Use a slotted spoon to transfer the cooked beef to a plate and set it aside.
5. In the same skillet, add the sliced bell pepper and onion. Stir-fry for 2-3 minutes until they are crisp-tender.
6. Return the cooked beef to the skillet with the vegetables. Stir in the Thai basil leaves and toss everything together until the basil wilts and is evenly distributed.
7. Remove the skillet from the heat and serve the Thai basil beef stir-fry immediately with cooked rice.
8. Enjoy your flavorful and aromatic Thai basil beef stir-fry!

This dish is best served hot and enjoyed immediately. The combination of tender beef, aromatic Thai basil, and savory sauce makes it a delicious and satisfying meal that's perfect for any day of the week.

Caprese Stuffed Chicken Breast

Ingredients:

- 4 boneless, skinless chicken breasts
- Salt and pepper, to taste
- 1 tablespoon olive oil
- 2 large tomatoes, sliced
- 8 ounces (225g) fresh mozzarella cheese, sliced
- 1/4 cup (10g) fresh basil leaves
- Balsamic glaze, for drizzling (optional)
- Toothpicks or kitchen twine, for securing the chicken breasts

Instructions:

1. Preheat your oven to 400°F (200°C).
2. Place each chicken breast between two sheets of plastic wrap or parchment paper. Use a meat mallet or rolling pin to pound the chicken breasts to an even thickness of about 1/2 inch.
3. Season each chicken breast with salt and pepper to taste on both sides.
4. Lay the chicken breasts flat on a work surface. Place a layer of tomato slices on one half of each chicken breast.
5. Top the tomatoes with slices of fresh mozzarella cheese.
6. Tear the fresh basil leaves and scatter them over the mozzarella cheese.
7. Fold the other half of each chicken breast over the filling to create a pocket. Secure the edges with toothpicks or tie with kitchen twine to keep the filling in place.
8. Heat olive oil in an oven-safe skillet over medium-high heat. Once hot, add the stuffed chicken breasts to the skillet.
9. Sear the chicken breasts for 2-3 minutes on each side until golden brown.
10. Transfer the skillet to the preheated oven and bake for 20-25 minutes, or until the chicken is cooked through and reaches an internal temperature of 165°F (75°C).
11. Once done, remove the skillet from the oven and let the chicken breasts rest for a few minutes before serving.
12. Optionally, drizzle the cooked chicken breasts with balsamic glaze before serving for extra flavor.

13. Serve the Caprese stuffed chicken breast hot, garnished with additional fresh basil leaves if desired.

Enjoy your delicious and flavorful Caprese stuffed chicken breast! It pairs well with a side salad, roasted vegetables, or your favorite grain.

Vegetarian Black Bean Enchiladas

Ingredients:

For the Enchilada Sauce:

- 2 tablespoons vegetable oil
- 2 tablespoons all-purpose flour
- 4 tablespoons chili powder
- 1 teaspoon ground cumin
- 1/2 teaspoon garlic powder
- 1/2 teaspoon onion powder
- 1/4 teaspoon dried oregano
- 2 cups (480ml) vegetable broth
- Salt and pepper, to taste

For the Filling:

- 1 tablespoon vegetable oil
- 1 small onion, diced
- 2 cloves garlic, minced
- 1 red bell pepper, diced
- 1 jalapeño pepper, seeded and minced (optional, for heat)
- 1 can (15 ounces/425g) black beans, drained and rinsed
- 1 cup (240ml) corn kernels (fresh, frozen, or canned)
- 1 teaspoon ground cumin
- 1 teaspoon chili powder
- Salt and pepper, to taste
- 1/4 cup (10g) chopped fresh cilantro
- 2 cups (200g) shredded cheese (such as cheddar or Monterey Jack)

For Assembling:

- 8-10 large flour tortillas
- Enchilada sauce (from the recipe above)

- Shredded cheese, for topping
- Chopped fresh cilantro, for garnish
- Sliced jalapeños, for garnish (optional)
- Sour cream, for serving (optional)
- Sliced avocado, for serving (optional)

Instructions:

1. Preheat your oven to 375°F (190°C). Grease a 9x13-inch baking dish and set aside.
2. To make the enchilada sauce, heat the vegetable oil in a saucepan over medium heat. Add the flour and whisk constantly for 1-2 minutes until it turns golden brown.
3. Stir in the chili powder, ground cumin, garlic powder, onion powder, and dried oregano. Cook for another minute until fragrant.
4. Gradually whisk in the vegetable broth, stirring constantly to prevent lumps from forming. Bring the sauce to a simmer and cook for 5-7 minutes until thickened. Season with salt and pepper to taste. Set aside.
5. To make the filling, heat the vegetable oil in a skillet over medium heat. Add the diced onion and cook for 2-3 minutes until softened.
6. Add the minced garlic, diced red bell pepper, and minced jalapeño pepper (if using). Cook for another 2-3 minutes until the peppers are tender.
7. Stir in the black beans, corn kernels, ground cumin, chili powder, salt, and pepper. Cook for 2-3 minutes until heated through. Remove from heat and stir in the chopped fresh cilantro.
8. To assemble the enchiladas, spoon a small amount of enchilada sauce onto the bottom of the prepared baking dish.
9. Place a spoonful of the black bean filling down the center of each tortilla. Roll up the tortillas and place them seam-side down in the baking dish.
10. Pour the remaining enchilada sauce over the rolled tortillas, making sure to cover them evenly.
11. Sprinkle shredded cheese over the top of the enchiladas.
12. Cover the baking dish with foil and bake in the preheated oven for 20-25 minutes until the enchiladas are heated through and the cheese is melted.
13. Remove the foil and bake for an additional 5-10 minutes until the cheese is bubbly and golden brown.
14. Garnish the enchiladas with chopped fresh cilantro and sliced jalapeños, if desired. Serve hot with sour cream and sliced avocado on the side, if desired.

15. Enjoy your delicious vegetarian black bean enchiladas as a flavorful and satisfying meal!

These enchiladas are packed with protein-rich black beans, flavorful spices, and gooey melted cheese, making them a crowd-pleasing favorite for vegetarians and meat-eaters alike.

Lemon Garlic Butter Shrimp with Zucchini Noodles

Ingredients:

For the Lemon Garlic Butter Shrimp:

- 1 lb (450g) large shrimp, peeled and deveined
- Salt and black pepper, to taste
- 2 tablespoons unsalted butter
- 4 cloves garlic, minced
- Zest of 1 lemon
- Juice of 1 lemon
- 1/4 cup (60ml) chicken broth or white wine
- 2 tablespoons chopped fresh parsley
- Crushed red pepper flakes, to taste (optional)

For the Zucchini Noodles (Zoodles):

- 4 medium zucchini
- 2 tablespoons olive oil
- Salt and black pepper, to taste
- Grated Parmesan cheese, for serving (optional)

Instructions:

1. Using a spiralizer, spiralize the zucchini into noodles. If you don't have a spiralizer, you can use a vegetable peeler to make thin ribbons or slice the zucchini into thin strips with a knife.
2. Season the shrimp with salt and black pepper to taste.
3. Heat 1 tablespoon of olive oil in a large skillet over medium-high heat. Add the shrimp in a single layer and cook for 1-2 minutes on each side until pink and cooked through. Remove the shrimp from the skillet and set aside.
4. In the same skillet, melt the butter over medium heat. Add the minced garlic and cook for 1 minute until fragrant.

5. Add the lemon zest, lemon juice, and chicken broth (or white wine) to the skillet. Stir to combine and bring to a simmer.
6. Return the cooked shrimp to the skillet and toss to coat them in the lemon garlic butter sauce. Cook for an additional 1-2 minutes until heated through.
7. Stir in the chopped parsley and crushed red pepper flakes (if using). Taste and adjust the seasoning with salt and black pepper if needed.
8. Meanwhile, heat the remaining 1 tablespoon of olive oil in another skillet over medium heat. Add the zucchini noodles and toss to coat them in the oil. Cook for 2-3 minutes until the noodles are just tender but still crisp.
9. Season the zucchini noodles with salt and black pepper to taste.
10. Divide the zucchini noodles among serving plates. Top with the lemon garlic butter shrimp.
11. Serve the lemon garlic butter shrimp with zucchini noodles hot, garnished with grated Parmesan cheese if desired.
12. Enjoy your light and flavorful meal!

This lemon garlic butter shrimp with zucchini noodles is a delicious and healthy option for a quick weeknight dinner. It's low-carb, gluten-free, and packed with fresh flavors that will satisfy your cravings without weighing you down.

One-Pot Chicken Alfredo Pasta

Ingredients:

- 1 lb (450g) boneless, skinless chicken breasts, cut into bite-sized pieces
- Salt and black pepper, to taste
- 2 tablespoons olive oil
- 4 cloves garlic, minced
- 2 cups (480ml) chicken broth
- 2 cups (480ml) water
- 12 ounces (340g) fettuccine pasta
- 1 cup (240ml) heavy cream
- 1/2 cup (50g) grated Parmesan cheese
- 1 cup (240g) frozen peas
- Chopped fresh parsley, for garnish (optional)

Instructions:

1. Season the chicken pieces with salt and black pepper to taste.
2. Heat the olive oil in a large skillet or pot over medium-high heat. Add the seasoned chicken pieces and cook for 5-6 minutes until they are browned and cooked through. Remove the chicken from the skillet and set aside.
3. In the same skillet, add the minced garlic and cook for 1 minute until fragrant.
4. Pour the chicken broth and water into the skillet and bring to a boil.
5. Add the fettuccine pasta to the boiling liquid and cook according to the package instructions, stirring occasionally to prevent sticking.
6. Once the pasta is almost cooked (about 8-10 minutes), reduce the heat to medium-low.
7. Stir in the heavy cream and grated Parmesan cheese until the cheese is melted and the sauce is creamy.
8. Return the cooked chicken to the skillet and add the frozen peas. Stir everything together and cook for an additional 2-3 minutes until the peas are heated through.
9. Taste and adjust the seasoning with salt and black pepper if needed.
10. Remove the skillet from the heat and garnish the chicken Alfredo pasta with chopped fresh parsley, if desired.
11. Serve the one-pot chicken Alfredo pasta hot, straight from the skillet.

12. Enjoy your creamy and comforting meal!

This one-pot chicken Alfredo pasta is a convenient and delicious option for a weeknight dinner. It's quick to prepare and requires minimal cleanup, making it perfect for busy evenings when you want a comforting and satisfying meal without spending hours in the kitchen.

Quinoa and Black Bean Stuffed Bell Peppers

Ingredients:

- 4 large bell peppers (any color), halved and seeds removed
- 1 cup (180g) quinoa, rinsed
- 2 cups (480ml) vegetable broth or water
- 1 tablespoon olive oil
- 1 small onion, finely chopped
- 2 cloves garlic, minced
- 1 can (15 ounces/425g) black beans, drained and rinsed
- 1 cup (150g) corn kernels (fresh, frozen, or canned)
- 1 teaspoon ground cumin
- 1 teaspoon chili powder
- Salt and black pepper, to taste
- 1 cup (120g) shredded cheese (cheddar, Monterey Jack, or a blend)
- Chopped fresh cilantro, for garnish (optional)
- Sour cream or Greek yogurt, for serving (optional)
- Sliced avocado, for serving (optional)

Instructions:

1. Preheat your oven to 375°F (190°C). Grease a baking dish large enough to hold the halved bell peppers.
2. In a medium saucepan, combine the quinoa and vegetable broth or water. Bring to a boil, then reduce the heat to low, cover, and simmer for 15-20 minutes until the quinoa is cooked and the liquid is absorbed. Remove from heat and set aside.
3. While the quinoa is cooking, heat olive oil in a large skillet over medium heat. Add the chopped onion and cook for 2-3 minutes until softened.
4. Add the minced garlic to the skillet and cook for another minute until fragrant.
5. Stir in the black beans, corn kernels, ground cumin, and chili powder. Cook for 3-4 minutes until heated through. Season with salt and black pepper to taste.
6. Remove the skillet from the heat and stir in the cooked quinoa until well combined.
7. Arrange the halved bell peppers in the prepared baking dish, cut side up.
8. Spoon the quinoa and black bean mixture evenly into each bell pepper half, pressing down gently to pack the filling.

9. Sprinkle shredded cheese over the top of each stuffed bell pepper.
10. Cover the baking dish with foil and bake in the preheated oven for 25-30 minutes until the peppers are tender and the cheese is melted and bubbly.
11. Remove the foil and bake for an additional 5-10 minutes until the cheese is golden brown.
12. Remove the stuffed bell peppers from the oven and let them cool slightly before serving.
13. Garnish the quinoa and black bean stuffed bell peppers with chopped fresh cilantro, if desired. Serve hot with sour cream or Greek yogurt and sliced avocado on the side, if desired.
14. Enjoy your nutritious and flavorful meal!

These quinoa and black bean stuffed bell peppers are packed with protein, fiber, and essential nutrients, making them a satisfying and wholesome meal option. They're also versatile, so feel free to customize the filling with your favorite vegetables and spices.

Sheet Pan Fajitas (Chicken or Beef)

Ingredients:

For the Fajita Seasoning:

- 2 teaspoons chili powder
- 1 teaspoon ground cumin
- 1 teaspoon smoked paprika
- 1/2 teaspoon garlic powder
- 1/2 teaspoon onion powder
- 1/4 teaspoon cayenne pepper (adjust to taste for spice level)
- Salt and black pepper, to taste

For the Sheet Pan Fajitas:

- 1 lb (450g) chicken breasts or beef steak, thinly sliced
- 2 bell peppers, thinly sliced
- 1 onion, thinly sliced
- 2 tablespoons vegetable oil or olive oil
- Juice of 1 lime
- Fresh cilantro, chopped, for garnish (optional)
- Tortillas, for serving
- Optional toppings: salsa, sour cream, guacamole, shredded cheese, sliced jalapeños, etc.

Instructions:

1. Preheat your oven to 400°F (200°C). Line a large baking sheet with parchment paper or aluminum foil for easy cleanup.
2. In a small bowl, mix together the fajita seasoning ingredients: chili powder, ground cumin, smoked paprika, garlic powder, onion powder, cayenne pepper, salt, and black pepper.
3. Place the thinly sliced chicken or beef, bell peppers, and onions on the prepared baking sheet.
4. Drizzle the vegetable oil or olive oil over the chicken or beef, bell peppers, and onions. Sprinkle the fajita seasoning evenly over everything.

5. Squeeze the lime juice over the ingredients on the baking sheet.
6. Use your hands or a spatula to toss everything together until the chicken or beef, bell peppers, and onions are evenly coated with the seasoning and oil.
7. Spread the ingredients out into an even layer on the baking sheet.
8. Bake in the preheated oven for 20-25 minutes, or until the chicken or beef is cooked through and the vegetables are tender and slightly caramelized, stirring halfway through.
9. Once done, remove the baking sheet from the oven.
10. Serve the sheet pan fajitas hot with warmed tortillas and optional toppings such as salsa, sour cream, guacamole, shredded cheese, sliced jalapeños, and chopped fresh cilantro.
11. Enjoy your delicious and flavorful sheet pan fajitas!

These sheet pan fajitas are versatile and customizable, making them a crowd-pleasing meal for the whole family. You can also adjust the seasoning and toppings according to your preferences.

Creamy Parmesan Garlic Mushroom Chicken

Ingredients:

- 4 boneless, skinless chicken breasts
- Salt and black pepper, to taste
- 2 tablespoons olive oil
- 8 ounces (225g) mushrooms, sliced
- 4 cloves garlic, minced
- 1 cup (240ml) chicken broth
- 1 cup (240ml) heavy cream
- 1/2 cup (50g) grated Parmesan cheese
- 1 teaspoon dried thyme (or 1 tablespoon fresh thyme leaves)
- Chopped fresh parsley, for garnish (optional)

Instructions:

1. Season the chicken breasts with salt and black pepper on both sides.
2. Heat olive oil in a large skillet over medium-high heat. Add the chicken breasts to the skillet and cook for 5-6 minutes on each side until golden brown and cooked through. Remove the chicken from the skillet and set aside.
3. In the same skillet, add the sliced mushrooms and cook for 4-5 minutes until they are golden brown and tender.
4. Add the minced garlic to the skillet and cook for 1 minute until fragrant.
5. Pour the chicken broth into the skillet and scrape up any browned bits from the bottom of the pan.
6. Stir in the heavy cream, grated Parmesan cheese, and dried thyme. Bring the mixture to a simmer and cook for 5-7 minutes until the sauce thickens slightly.
7. Return the cooked chicken breasts to the skillet and spoon some of the sauce over the top.
8. Let the chicken simmer in the sauce for another 2-3 minutes until heated through and the flavors meld together.
9. Once done, remove the skillet from the heat and garnish the creamy Parmesan garlic mushroom chicken with chopped fresh parsley, if desired.
10. Serve the chicken hot, with extra sauce spooned over the top.
11. Enjoy your creamy and flavorful meal!

This creamy Parmesan garlic mushroom chicken is delicious served over pasta, rice, or mashed potatoes, with a side of steamed vegetables or a crisp green salad. It's sure to become a favorite in your recipe rotation!

Spicy Peanut Noodles with Vegetables

Ingredients:

For the Peanut Sauce:

- 1/4 cup (60ml) soy sauce
- 3 tablespoons smooth peanut butter
- 2 tablespoons rice vinegar
- 1 tablespoon sesame oil
- 1 tablespoon honey or maple syrup
- 2 cloves garlic, minced
- 1 teaspoon grated ginger
- 1-2 teaspoons sriracha or chili garlic sauce (adjust to taste)
- 2-4 tablespoons water, to thin the sauce

For the Noodles and Vegetables:

- 8 ounces (225g) spaghetti or noodles of your choice
- 2 tablespoons vegetable oil
- 2 bell peppers, thinly sliced
- 1 medium carrot, julienned or grated
- 1 cup (150g) shredded cabbage
- 1/2 cup (75g) edamame (optional)
- 2 green onions, thinly sliced
- Sesame seeds, for garnish (optional)
- Chopped fresh cilantro or parsley, for garnish (optional)
- Lime wedges, for serving (optional)

Instructions:

1. Cook the spaghetti or noodles according to the package instructions until al dente. Drain and set aside.
2. In a small bowl, whisk together all the ingredients for the peanut sauce: soy sauce, peanut butter, rice vinegar, sesame oil, honey or maple syrup, minced

garlic, grated ginger, and sriracha or chili garlic sauce. If the sauce is too thick, add 2-4 tablespoons of water to thin it out to your desired consistency. Set the sauce aside.
3. Heat vegetable oil in a large skillet or wok over medium-high heat. Add the sliced bell peppers and julienned carrots to the skillet. Stir-fry for 2-3 minutes until they start to soften.
4. Add the shredded cabbage and edamame (if using) to the skillet. Continue to stir-fry for another 2-3 minutes until the vegetables are tender-crisp.
5. Add the cooked noodles to the skillet along with the prepared peanut sauce. Toss everything together until the noodles and vegetables are evenly coated in the sauce.
6. Cook for an additional 1-2 minutes, stirring constantly, until everything is heated through.
7. Remove the skillet from the heat and garnish the spicy peanut noodles with thinly sliced green onions, sesame seeds, and chopped fresh cilantro or parsley, if desired.
8. Serve the spicy peanut noodles with vegetables hot, with lime wedges on the side for squeezing over the noodles, if desired.
9. Enjoy your delicious and flavorful meal!

These spicy peanut noodles with vegetables are versatile and customizable, so feel free to add your favorite veggies or protein sources to make it your own. They're perfect for a quick weeknight dinner or meal prep for lunch the next day.

Baked Teriyaki Salmon with Broccoli

Ingredients:

For the Teriyaki Sauce:

- 1/4 cup (60ml) soy sauce
- 2 tablespoons honey
- 1 tablespoon rice vinegar
- 1 clove garlic, minced
- 1 teaspoon grated ginger
- 1 teaspoon cornstarch
- 1 tablespoon water

For the Salmon and Broccoli:

- 4 salmon fillets (about 6 ounces/170g each), skin-on or skinless
- Salt and black pepper, to taste
- 4 cups broccoli florets
- 2 tablespoons olive oil
- Sesame seeds, for garnish (optional)
- Sliced green onions, for garnish (optional)

Instructions:

1. Preheat your oven to 400°F (200°C). Line a baking sheet with parchment paper or aluminum foil for easy cleanup.
2. In a small saucepan, combine the soy sauce, honey, rice vinegar, minced garlic, and grated ginger. Heat the sauce over medium heat, stirring occasionally, until it comes to a simmer.
3. In a small bowl, mix together the cornstarch and water to create a slurry. Stir the slurry into the simmering sauce and continue to cook for another 1-2 minutes until the sauce thickens. Remove from heat and set aside.
4. Place the salmon fillets on the prepared baking sheet. Season them with salt and black pepper to taste.

5. In a large bowl, toss the broccoli florets with olive oil until they are evenly coated. Season the broccoli with salt and black pepper to taste.
6. Arrange the broccoli around the salmon fillets on the baking sheet in a single layer.
7. Brush the teriyaki sauce over the salmon fillets, reserving some sauce for serving.
8. Bake in the preheated oven for 12-15 minutes, or until the salmon is cooked through and flakes easily with a fork, and the broccoli is tender-crisp.
9. Once done, remove the baking sheet from the oven. Drizzle the remaining teriyaki sauce over the salmon and broccoli.
10. Garnish the baked teriyaki salmon and broccoli with sesame seeds and sliced green onions, if desired.
11. Serve hot, with steamed rice or quinoa on the side, if desired.
12. Enjoy your delicious and nutritious baked teriyaki salmon with broccoli!

This dish is not only flavorful and satisfying but also packed with protein from the salmon and fiber and vitamins from the broccoli, making it a wholesome meal option for any day of the week.

Veggie-Packed Turkey Meatballs with Marinara Sauce

Ingredients:

For the Turkey Meatballs:

- 1 lb (450g) lean ground turkey
- 1 cup grated zucchini (about 1 medium zucchini)
- 1 cup grated carrot (about 2 medium carrots)
- 1/4 cup finely chopped onion
- 2 cloves garlic, minced
- 1/4 cup breadcrumbs
- 1/4 cup grated Parmesan cheese
- 1 large egg
- 1 tablespoon chopped fresh parsley (or 1 teaspoon dried parsley)
- 1 teaspoon dried oregano
- 1/2 teaspoon salt
- 1/4 teaspoon black pepper
- Olive oil, for cooking

For the Marinara Sauce:

- 1 tablespoon olive oil
- 1 small onion, finely chopped
- 2 cloves garlic, minced
- 1 can (14 ounces/400g) crushed tomatoes
- 1 can (8 ounces/225g) tomato sauce
- 1 teaspoon dried basil
- 1 teaspoon dried oregano
- Salt and black pepper, to taste

Instructions:

1. Preheat your oven to 400°F (200°C). Line a baking sheet with parchment paper or aluminum foil for easy cleanup.
2. In a large mixing bowl, combine the ground turkey, grated zucchini, grated carrot, finely chopped onion, minced garlic, breadcrumbs, grated Parmesan cheese, egg,

chopped parsley, dried oregano, salt, and black pepper. Mix everything together until well combined.
3. Shape the turkey mixture into meatballs, about 1 to 1.5 inches in diameter, and place them on the prepared baking sheet.
4. Drizzle a little olive oil over the meatballs to help them brown in the oven.
5. Bake the meatballs in the preheated oven for 20-25 minutes, or until they are cooked through and lightly browned on the outside.
6. While the meatballs are baking, prepare the marinara sauce. Heat olive oil in a saucepan over medium heat. Add the finely chopped onion and cook for 2-3 minutes until softened.
7. Add the minced garlic to the saucepan and cook for another minute until fragrant.
8. Stir in the crushed tomatoes, tomato sauce, dried basil, and dried oregano. Season with salt and black pepper to taste.
9. Bring the sauce to a simmer, then reduce the heat to low and let it simmer gently for 15-20 minutes, stirring occasionally, to allow the flavors to meld together.
10. Once the meatballs are done baking and the marinara sauce is ready, serve the meatballs hot with the marinara sauce spooned over the top.
11. Enjoy your veggie-packed turkey meatballs with marinara sauce, served over cooked pasta or alongside your favorite side dishes!

These meatballs are not only flavorful and satisfying but also packed with veggies, making them a wholesome and nutritious option for a family dinner.

Lemon Herb Grilled Chicken with Quinoa

Ingredients:

For the Lemon Herb Marinade:

- 1/4 cup olive oil
- Zest of 1 lemon
- Juice of 1 lemon
- 2 cloves garlic, minced
- 1 tablespoon chopped fresh herbs (such as parsley, thyme, rosemary, or basil)
- 1 teaspoon dried oregano
- Salt and black pepper, to taste

For the Grilled Chicken:

- 4 boneless, skinless chicken breasts
- Lemon wedges, for serving

For the Quinoa:

- 1 cup quinoa
- 2 cups water or chicken broth
- Salt, to taste
- Chopped fresh parsley or cilantro, for garnish (optional)

Instructions:

1. In a small bowl, whisk together the olive oil, lemon zest, lemon juice, minced garlic, chopped fresh herbs, dried oregano, salt, and black pepper to make the marinade.
2. Place the chicken breasts in a shallow dish or resealable plastic bag. Pour the marinade over the chicken, making sure it's evenly coated. Cover the dish or seal the bag, then refrigerate for at least 30 minutes or up to 4 hours to marinate.

3. While the chicken is marinating, rinse the quinoa under cold water using a fine mesh sieve. In a medium saucepan, combine the quinoa and water or chicken broth. Bring to a boil, then reduce the heat to low, cover, and simmer for 15-20 minutes, or until the quinoa is cooked and the liquid is absorbed. Fluff the quinoa with a fork and season with salt to taste. Keep warm.
4. Preheat your grill to medium-high heat. Remove the chicken breasts from the marinade and discard any excess marinade.
5. Grill the chicken breasts for 6-8 minutes per side, or until they are cooked through and have reached an internal temperature of 165°F (75°C). Cooking time may vary depending on the thickness of the chicken breasts.
6. Once the chicken is done, remove it from the grill and let it rest for a few minutes before slicing.
7. To serve, divide the cooked quinoa among serving plates. Top with sliced grilled chicken breasts. Garnish with chopped fresh parsley or cilantro, if desired. Serve with lemon wedges on the side for squeezing over the chicken.
8. Enjoy your delicious lemon herb grilled chicken with quinoa!

This dish is not only flavorful and satisfying but also packed with protein, fiber, and essential nutrients, making it a wholesome and nutritious option for a balanced meal.

Creamy Tuscan Garlic Chicken

Ingredients:

- 4 boneless, skinless chicken breasts
- Salt and black pepper, to taste
- 2 tablespoons olive oil
- 4 cloves garlic, minced
- 1 cup (240ml) chicken broth
- 1 cup (240ml) heavy cream
- 1/2 cup (50g) grated Parmesan cheese
- 1 teaspoon dried thyme (or 1 tablespoon fresh thyme leaves)
- 1 teaspoon dried oregano
- 1/2 cup sun-dried tomatoes, drained and chopped
- 2 cups baby spinach leaves
- Chopped fresh parsley, for garnish (optional)

Instructions:

1. Season the chicken breasts with salt and black pepper on both sides.
2. Heat olive oil in a large skillet over medium-high heat. Add the seasoned chicken breasts to the skillet and cook for 5-6 minutes on each side until golden brown and cooked through. Remove the chicken from the skillet and set aside.
3. In the same skillet, add the minced garlic and cook for 1-2 minutes until fragrant.
4. Pour the chicken broth into the skillet and use a spatula to scrape up any browned bits from the bottom of the pan.
5. Stir in the heavy cream, grated Parmesan cheese, dried thyme, and dried oregano. Bring the mixture to a simmer and cook for 2-3 minutes until the sauce thickens slightly.
6. Stir in the chopped sun-dried tomatoes and baby spinach leaves. Cook for another 1-2 minutes until the spinach wilts.
7. Return the cooked chicken breasts to the skillet and spoon some of the sauce over the top.
8. Let the chicken simmer in the sauce for another 2-3 minutes until heated through and the flavors meld together.
9. Once done, remove the skillet from the heat and garnish the creamy Tuscan garlic chicken with chopped fresh parsley, if desired.
10. Serve the chicken hot, with extra sauce spooned over the top.

11. Enjoy your creamy and flavorful meal!

This creamy Tuscan garlic chicken pairs well with cooked pasta, rice, or mashed potatoes, with a side of steamed vegetables or a crisp green salad. It's sure to become a favorite in your recipe rotation!

Black Bean and Corn Quesadillas

Ingredients:

- 1 can (15 ounces/425g) black beans, drained and rinsed
- 1 cup frozen corn kernels, thawed
- 1/2 cup diced bell peppers (any color)
- 1/4 cup chopped fresh cilantro
- 1 teaspoon ground cumin
- 1/2 teaspoon chili powder
- Salt and black pepper, to taste
- 4 large flour tortillas
- 1 cup shredded cheese (such as cheddar, Monterey Jack, or a blend)
- Olive oil or cooking spray, for cooking
- Optional toppings: salsa, guacamole, sour cream, chopped fresh cilantro, sliced jalapeños, etc.

Instructions:

1. In a large mixing bowl, combine the black beans, corn kernels, diced bell peppers, chopped cilantro, ground cumin, chili powder, salt, and black pepper. Stir until well combined.
2. Place a large skillet or griddle over medium heat. Brush one side of a flour tortilla with a little olive oil or spray it lightly with cooking spray. Place the tortilla, oiled side down, in the skillet.
3. Spoon some of the black bean and corn mixture onto half of the tortilla, spreading it evenly. Sprinkle some shredded cheese over the top of the bean mixture.
4. Fold the other half of the tortilla over the filling to create a half-moon shape.
5. Cook the quesadilla for 2-3 minutes on each side, or until it is golden brown and crispy, and the cheese is melted.
6. Repeat the process with the remaining tortillas and filling.
7. Once done, remove the quesadillas from the skillet and let them cool for a minute or two before slicing them into wedges.
8. Serve the black bean and corn quesadillas hot, with your favorite toppings such as salsa, guacamole, sour cream, chopped fresh cilantro, or sliced jalapeños on the side.

9. Enjoy your delicious and flavorful meal!

These black bean and corn quesadillas are perfect for a quick lunch or dinner, and they're also great for meal prep. They're packed with protein and fiber from the beans and corn, making them a nutritious and satisfying option for vegetarians and meat-eaters alike.

Honey Sriracha Chicken with Rice

Ingredients:

For the Honey Sriracha Sauce:

- 1/4 cup honey
- 2 tablespoons Sriracha sauce (adjust to taste for spice level)
- 2 tablespoons soy sauce
- 1 tablespoon rice vinegar
- 2 cloves garlic, minced
- 1 teaspoon grated ginger
- 1 tablespoon cornstarch
- 2 tablespoons water

For the Chicken:

- 1 lb (450g) boneless, skinless chicken breasts, cut into bite-sized pieces
- Salt and black pepper, to taste
- 2 tablespoons vegetable oil
- Cooked rice, for serving
- Optional garnishes: sliced green onions, sesame seeds, chopped cilantro

Instructions:

1. In a small bowl, whisk together the honey, Sriracha sauce, soy sauce, rice vinegar, minced garlic, and grated ginger to make the sauce.
2. In a separate small bowl, mix together the cornstarch and water to create a slurry.
3. Season the bite-sized chicken pieces with salt and black pepper.
4. Heat the vegetable oil in a large skillet or wok over medium-high heat. Add the seasoned chicken pieces to the skillet and cook for 5-6 minutes, or until they are golden brown and cooked through.
5. Pour the prepared Honey Sriracha sauce over the cooked chicken in the skillet. Stir to coat the chicken evenly in the sauce.

6. Stir the cornstarch slurry to recombine, then pour it into the skillet with the chicken and sauce. Stir everything together and cook for another 1-2 minutes, or until the sauce thickens.
7. Once done, remove the skillet from the heat.
8. Serve the Honey Sriracha chicken hot, over cooked rice.
9. Garnish with sliced green onions, sesame seeds, and chopped cilantro, if desired.
10. Enjoy your delicious and flavorful Honey Sriracha chicken with rice!

This dish is perfect for a quick and satisfying weeknight dinner. It's packed with bold flavors and can be customized to your taste preferences by adjusting the amount of Sriracha sauce used.

Spinach and Ricotta Stuffed Shells

Ingredients:

For the Stuffed Shells:

- 12 ounces (340g) jumbo pasta shells
- 2 cups ricotta cheese
- 1 1/2 cups shredded mozzarella cheese, divided
- 1/2 cup grated Parmesan cheese
- 1 large egg
- 1 teaspoon dried basil
- 1 teaspoon dried oregano
- 1/2 teaspoon garlic powder
- 1/2 teaspoon onion powder
- Salt and black pepper, to taste
- 1 cup frozen chopped spinach, thawed and squeezed dry
- 2 cups marinara sauce

Instructions:

1. Preheat your oven to 375°F (190°C). Grease a 9x13-inch baking dish with non-stick cooking spray.
2. Cook the jumbo pasta shells according to the package instructions until al dente. Drain and set aside to cool slightly.
3. In a large mixing bowl, combine the ricotta cheese, 1 cup of shredded mozzarella cheese, grated Parmesan cheese, egg, dried basil, dried oregano, garlic powder, onion powder, salt, and black pepper. Mix until well combined.
4. Stir in the thawed and squeezed dry chopped spinach until evenly distributed throughout the cheese mixture.
5. Spoon about 2 tablespoons of the spinach and ricotta mixture into each cooked pasta shell, filling them evenly.
6. Spread 1 cup of marinara sauce evenly over the bottom of the prepared baking dish.
7. Arrange the stuffed shells in the baking dish in a single layer.

8. Pour the remaining marinara sauce over the top of the stuffed shells, spreading it evenly to cover them.
9. Sprinkle the remaining 1/2 cup of shredded mozzarella cheese over the top of the stuffed shells.
10. Cover the baking dish with aluminum foil and bake in the preheated oven for 25-30 minutes, or until the cheese is melted and bubbly.
11. Once done, remove the foil and bake for an additional 5-10 minutes, or until the cheese is golden brown.
12. Remove the stuffed shells from the oven and let them cool for a few minutes before serving.
13. Serve the spinach and ricotta stuffed shells hot, garnished with chopped fresh basil or parsley, if desired.
14. Enjoy your comforting and delicious Italian-inspired meal!

These spinach and ricotta stuffed shells are perfect for a family dinner or a special occasion. They're hearty, flavorful, and sure to be a hit with everyone at the table.

Moroccan Chickpea Stew

Ingredients:

- 2 tablespoons olive oil
- 1 large onion, chopped
- 3 cloves garlic, minced
- 1 tablespoon ground cumin
- 1 tablespoon ground coriander
- 1 teaspoon ground turmeric
- 1 teaspoon ground cinnamon
- 1/2 teaspoon ground ginger
- 1/4 teaspoon ground cloves
- 1/4 teaspoon cayenne pepper (adjust to taste)
- 1 can (14 ounces/400g) diced tomatoes
- 2 cans (14 ounces/400g each) chickpeas, drained and rinsed
- 2 cups vegetable broth
- 1 cup diced carrots
- 1 cup diced potatoes
- 1 cup diced zucchini
- 1 cup chopped kale or spinach
- Salt and black pepper, to taste
- Fresh cilantro, chopped, for garnish
- Lemon wedges, for serving
- Cooked couscous or rice, for serving (optional)

Instructions:

1. Heat olive oil in a large pot or Dutch oven over medium heat. Add the chopped onion and cook for 5 minutes, or until softened.
2. Add the minced garlic and cook for another minute until fragrant.
3. Stir in the ground cumin, ground coriander, ground turmeric, ground cinnamon, ground ginger, ground cloves, and cayenne pepper. Cook for 1-2 minutes until the spices are fragrant.
4. Add the diced tomatoes (with their juices), drained and rinsed chickpeas, vegetable broth, diced carrots, and diced potatoes to the pot. Stir to combine.

5. Bring the stew to a simmer, then reduce the heat to low and cover. Let it simmer for 20-25 minutes, or until the carrots and potatoes are tender.
6. Once the vegetables are tender, stir in the diced zucchini and chopped kale or spinach. Cook for an additional 5 minutes until the zucchini is tender and the kale/spinach is wilted.
7. Season the stew with salt and black pepper to taste.
8. Serve the Moroccan chickpea stew hot, garnished with chopped fresh cilantro and lemon wedges.
9. Optionally, serve the stew over cooked couscous or rice for a complete meal.
10. Enjoy your flavorful and comforting Moroccan chickpea stew!

This stew is not only delicious but also packed with protein, fiber, and essential nutrients from the chickpeas and vegetables. It's perfect for a cozy dinner on a chilly evening.

Garlic Butter Steak Bites with Potatoes

Ingredients:

For the Garlic Butter Steak Bites:

- 1 lb (450g) sirloin steak, trimmed and cut into bite-sized pieces
- Salt and black pepper, to taste
- 2 tablespoons olive oil
- 4 tablespoons unsalted butter
- 4 cloves garlic, minced
- 1 tablespoon chopped fresh parsley (optional)
- Lemon wedges, for serving

For the Potatoes:

- 1 lb (450g) baby potatoes, halved or quartered
- 2 tablespoons olive oil
- 1 teaspoon garlic powder
- 1 teaspoon paprika
- Salt and black pepper, to taste
- Chopped fresh parsley, for garnish (optional)

Instructions:

1. Preheat your oven to 425°F (220°C). Line a baking sheet with parchment paper or aluminum foil for easy cleanup.
2. Place the baby potatoes in a large mixing bowl. Drizzle with olive oil and sprinkle with garlic powder, paprika, salt, and black pepper. Toss until the potatoes are evenly coated.
3. Spread the seasoned potatoes out onto the prepared baking sheet in a single layer. Roast in the preheated oven for 20-25 minutes, or until the potatoes are tender and golden brown, stirring halfway through cooking.
4. While the potatoes are roasting, season the bite-sized pieces of sirloin steak with salt and black pepper to taste.
5. Heat olive oil in a large skillet over medium-high heat. Add the seasoned steak pieces to the skillet in a single layer, making sure not to overcrowd the pan. Cook

for 2-3 minutes per side, or until browned and cooked to your desired level of doneness. Remove the cooked steak bites from the skillet and set aside.
6. In the same skillet, melt the unsalted butter over medium heat. Add the minced garlic to the skillet and cook for 1-2 minutes until fragrant.
7. Return the cooked steak bites to the skillet with the garlic butter. Toss everything together until the steak bites are coated evenly in the garlic butter sauce. Cook for another minute, stirring occasionally, to heat through.
8. Once done, remove the skillet from the heat and sprinkle the steak bites with chopped fresh parsley, if desired.
9. Serve the garlic butter steak bites hot, with roasted potatoes on the side. Garnish with additional chopped fresh parsley and lemon wedges for squeezing over the steak bites, if desired.
10. Enjoy your delicious and flavorful garlic butter steak bites with potatoes!

This dish is perfect for a hearty and satisfying dinner, and it's sure to become a family favorite.

Vegetable Stir-Fry with Tofu

Ingredients:

For the Stir-Fry Sauce:

- 1/4 cup soy sauce
- 2 tablespoons rice vinegar
- 1 tablespoon honey or maple syrup
- 1 tablespoon sesame oil
- 2 cloves garlic, minced
- 1 teaspoon grated ginger
- 1 teaspoon cornstarch
- 2 tablespoons water

For the Stir-Fry:

- 14 oz (400g) extra-firm tofu, pressed and cubed
- 2 tablespoons soy sauce
- 2 tablespoons cornstarch
- 2 tablespoons vegetable oil, divided
- 1 bell pepper, sliced
- 1 carrot, julienned or thinly sliced
- 1 cup broccoli florets
- 1 cup snow peas or snap peas
- 1 cup sliced mushrooms
- 2 green onions, chopped
- Cooked rice or noodles, for serving

Instructions:

1. In a small bowl, whisk together all the ingredients for the stir-fry sauce: soy sauce, rice vinegar, honey or maple syrup, sesame oil, minced garlic, grated ginger, cornstarch, and water. Set aside.

2. Press the tofu to remove excess moisture: Wrap the tofu in a clean kitchen towel and place a heavy object (such as a cast-iron skillet or a stack of plates) on top. Let it press for 15-20 minutes, then cut it into cubes.
3. In a shallow dish, combine the cubed tofu with soy sauce and cornstarch. Toss gently to coat.
4. Heat 1 tablespoon of vegetable oil in a large skillet or wok over medium-high heat. Add the tofu cubes and cook for 5-7 minutes, stirring occasionally, until golden brown and crispy. Remove the tofu from the skillet and set aside.
5. In the same skillet, add the remaining tablespoon of vegetable oil. Add the sliced bell pepper, julienned carrot, broccoli florets, snow peas or snap peas, and sliced mushrooms. Stir-fry for 4-5 minutes, or until the vegetables are tender-crisp.
6. Return the cooked tofu to the skillet with the vegetables. Pour the stir-fry sauce over the tofu and vegetables. Stir everything together and cook for another 1-2 minutes until the sauce thickens slightly and coats the tofu and vegetables.
7. Once done, remove the skillet from the heat and stir in the chopped green onions.
8. Serve the vegetable stir-fry with tofu hot, over cooked rice or noodles.
9. Enjoy your delicious and nutritious vegetable stir-fry with tofu!

Feel free to customize this recipe by adding your favorite vegetables or adjusting the seasoning to suit your taste preferences. It's a versatile and satisfying dish that's perfect for a quick weeknight dinner.

One-Pot Cajun Pasta

Ingredients:

- 8 oz (225g) pasta (such as penne, fusilli, or rigatoni)
- 1 tablespoon olive oil
- 1 lb (450g) chicken breast, cut into bite-sized pieces
- Salt and black pepper, to taste
- 1 tablespoon Cajun seasoning
- 1 onion, chopped
- 1 bell pepper, diced
- 2 cloves garlic, minced
- 1 can (14 oz/400g) diced tomatoes
- 2 cups chicken broth
- 1 cup heavy cream
- 1/2 cup grated Parmesan cheese
- Chopped fresh parsley, for garnish (optional)

Instructions:

1. In a large pot or Dutch oven, heat olive oil over medium-high heat. Add the chicken breast pieces to the pot and season with salt, black pepper, and Cajun seasoning. Cook for 5-6 minutes, or until the chicken is browned and cooked through. Remove the chicken from the pot and set aside.
2. In the same pot, add a little more olive oil if needed. Add the chopped onion and diced bell pepper to the pot and cook for 3-4 minutes, or until softened.
3. Add the minced garlic to the pot and cook for another minute until fragrant.
4. Stir in the diced tomatoes (with their juices), chicken broth, heavy cream, and cooked chicken pieces. Bring the mixture to a boil.
5. Once boiling, add the pasta to the pot. Stir to combine, making sure the pasta is submerged in the liquid.
6. Reduce the heat to medium-low and simmer, uncovered, for 10-12 minutes, stirring occasionally, or until the pasta is cooked al dente and the sauce has thickened.
7. Once the pasta is cooked, stir in the grated Parmesan cheese until melted and well combined.

8. Remove the pot from the heat and let the pasta sit for a few minutes to thicken up.
9. Serve the Cajun pasta hot, garnished with chopped fresh parsley if desired.
10. Enjoy your delicious one-pot Cajun pasta!

This dish is packed with flavor from the Cajun seasoning and is sure to become a favorite in your recipe rotation. Plus, since it's made in just one pot, cleanup is a breeze!

Baked Lemon Herb Cod with Green Beans

Ingredients:

- 4 cod fillets (about 6 ounces/170g each)
- Salt and black pepper, to taste
- 2 tablespoons olive oil
- 2 cloves garlic, minced
- Zest of 1 lemon
- 2 tablespoons lemon juice
- 1 tablespoon chopped fresh parsley
- 1 tablespoon chopped fresh dill (or 1 teaspoon dried dill)
- 1 tablespoon chopped fresh chives (or 1 teaspoon dried chives)
- 1 lb (450g) green beans, trimmed
- Lemon slices, for garnish (optional)

Instructions:

1. Preheat your oven to 400°F (200°C). Grease a baking dish with olive oil or cooking spray.
2. Pat the cod fillets dry with paper towels. Season both sides of the cod fillets with salt and black pepper to taste.
3. In a small bowl, whisk together the olive oil, minced garlic, lemon zest, lemon juice, chopped parsley, chopped dill, and chopped chives to make the lemon herb marinade.
4. Place the cod fillets in the prepared baking dish. Pour the lemon herb marinade over the cod fillets, making sure they are evenly coated.
5. Arrange the trimmed green beans around the cod fillets in the baking dish.
6. Drizzle a little more olive oil over the green beans and season them with salt and black pepper to taste.
7. Bake in the preheated oven for 15-20 minutes, or until the cod is opaque and flakes easily with a fork, and the green beans are tender-crisp.
8. Once done, remove the baking dish from the oven. If desired, garnish the baked lemon herb cod with lemon slices for serving.
9. Serve the baked lemon herb cod hot, with green beans on the side.
10. Enjoy your light and flavorful meal!

This baked lemon herb cod with green beans is perfect for a healthy and satisfying dinner. The combination of fresh herbs and lemon adds brightness to the dish, while the cod remains tender and flaky. It's a delicious and nutritious option for any day of the week.

Creamy Pesto Pasta with Cherry Tomatoes

Ingredients:

- 12 oz (340g) pasta (such as penne, fusilli, or spaghetti)
- 1 tablespoon olive oil
- 1 pint (about 2 cups) cherry tomatoes, halved
- Salt and black pepper, to taste
- 2 cloves garlic, minced
- 1/2 cup pesto sauce (store-bought or homemade)
- 1/2 cup heavy cream or half-and-half
- 1/4 cup grated Parmesan cheese
- Fresh basil leaves, chopped, for garnish (optional)

Instructions:

1. Cook the pasta according to the package instructions in a large pot of salted boiling water until al dente. Drain and set aside, reserving 1/2 cup of pasta cooking water.
2. While the pasta is cooking, heat olive oil in a large skillet over medium heat. Add the halved cherry tomatoes to the skillet and season with salt and black pepper to taste. Cook for 4-5 minutes, or until the tomatoes are softened and start to release their juices.
3. Add the minced garlic to the skillet with the cherry tomatoes and cook for another minute until fragrant.
4. Stir in the pesto sauce and heavy cream (or half-and-half) into the skillet with the tomatoes and garlic. Cook for 2-3 minutes, stirring occasionally, until the sauce is heated through.
5. Add the cooked pasta to the skillet with the creamy pesto sauce. Toss everything together until the pasta is evenly coated in the sauce, adding some of the reserved pasta cooking water as needed to loosen the sauce.
6. Once the pasta is coated in the sauce and heated through, sprinkle grated Parmesan cheese over the top. Stir to combine.
7. Once done, remove the skillet from the heat.
8. Serve the creamy pesto pasta hot, garnished with chopped fresh basil leaves, if desired.
9. Enjoy your delicious and comforting meal!

This creamy pesto pasta with cherry tomatoes is perfect for a quick and satisfying dinner. The combination of fresh tomatoes, garlic, basil pesto, and creamy sauce creates a flavorful and comforting dish that's sure to be a hit with the whole family.

Teriyaki Veggie Stir-Fry

Ingredients:

For the Teriyaki Sauce:

- 1/4 cup soy sauce
- 2 tablespoons water
- 2 tablespoons honey or maple syrup
- 1 tablespoon rice vinegar
- 1 clove garlic, minced
- 1 teaspoon grated ginger
- 1 teaspoon cornstarch
- 1 tablespoon water

For the Stir-Fry:

- 2 tablespoons sesame oil or vegetable oil
- 1 onion, thinly sliced
- 2 bell peppers, thinly sliced
- 2 carrots, julienned or thinly sliced
- 1 cup broccoli florets
- 1 cup snap peas or snow peas
- 1 cup sliced mushrooms
- 1 cup tofu, diced (optional)
- Cooked rice or noodles, for serving

Instructions:

1. In a small bowl, whisk together the soy sauce, water, honey or maple syrup, rice vinegar, minced garlic, and grated ginger to make the teriyaki sauce.
2. In another small bowl, mix together the cornstarch and water to make a slurry.
3. Heat sesame oil or vegetable oil in a large skillet or wok over medium-high heat. Add the thinly sliced onion to the skillet and cook for 2-3 minutes until softened.

4. Add the sliced bell peppers, julienned carrots, broccoli florets, snap peas or snow peas, and sliced mushrooms to the skillet. Stir-fry for 5-6 minutes, or until the vegetables are tender-crisp.
5. If using tofu, add the diced tofu to the skillet with the vegetables and cook for another 2-3 minutes, or until heated through.
6. Pour the prepared teriyaki sauce over the vegetables and tofu in the skillet. Stir to coat evenly.
7. Give the cornstarch slurry a quick stir to recombine, then pour it into the skillet. Stir-fry for another 1-2 minutes, or until the sauce thickens slightly.
8. Once done, remove the skillet from the heat.
9. Serve the teriyaki veggie stir-fry hot, over cooked rice or noodles.
10. Enjoy your delicious and nutritious teriyaki veggie stir-fry!

This dish is versatile, so feel free to customize it with your favorite vegetables or protein options. It's a satisfying and flavorful meal that's perfect for a quick and healthy dinner.

Italian Sausage and Peppers with Polenta

Ingredients:

For the Italian Sausage and Peppers:

- 1 lb (450g) Italian sausage links (sweet or hot), sliced
- 2 tablespoons olive oil
- 1 onion, thinly sliced
- 2 bell peppers (any color), thinly sliced
- 3 cloves garlic, minced
- 1 teaspoon dried oregano
- 1 teaspoon dried basil
- Salt and black pepper, to taste
- 1 can (14 oz/400g) diced tomatoes
- 1/2 cup chicken broth or water
- Chopped fresh parsley, for garnish (optional)

For the Polenta:

- 1 cup polenta or cornmeal
- 4 cups water or chicken broth
- Salt, to taste
- 1/2 cup grated Parmesan cheese
- 2 tablespoons unsalted butter

Instructions:

1. In a large skillet or Dutch oven, heat olive oil over medium heat. Add the sliced Italian sausage links to the skillet and cook until browned on all sides, about 5-7 minutes. Remove the sausage from the skillet and set aside.
2. In the same skillet, add a little more olive oil if needed. Add the thinly sliced onion and bell peppers to the skillet. Cook for 5-6 minutes, or until the vegetables are softened and lightly caramelized.
3. Add the minced garlic, dried oregano, and dried basil to the skillet with the onions and peppers. Cook for another minute until the garlic is fragrant.

4. Return the cooked Italian sausage to the skillet. Stir in the diced tomatoes (with their juices) and chicken broth or water. Season with salt and black pepper to taste.
5. Bring the mixture to a simmer, then reduce the heat to low. Cover and let it simmer for 20-25 minutes, stirring occasionally, until the sausage is cooked through and the flavors have melded together.
6. While the sausage and peppers are simmering, prepare the polenta. In a medium saucepan, bring the water or chicken broth to a boil. Gradually whisk in the polenta or cornmeal, stirring constantly to prevent lumps from forming.
7. Reduce the heat to low and simmer the polenta, stirring frequently, for 15-20 minutes, or until thickened and creamy. Stir in the grated Parmesan cheese and unsalted butter until melted and well combined. Season with salt to taste.
8. Once the sausage and peppers are done simmering and the polenta is ready, serve the sausage and peppers over the creamy polenta.
9. Garnish with chopped fresh parsley, if desired.
10. Enjoy your delicious Italian sausage and peppers with polenta!

This dish is perfect for a cozy and satisfying dinner, and it's sure to become a family favorite. The combination of savory Italian sausage, sweet bell peppers, and creamy polenta is simply irresistible.

Shrimp Scampi with Linguine

Ingredients:

- 12 oz (340g) linguine pasta
- 1 lb (450g) large shrimp, peeled and deveined
- Salt and black pepper, to taste
- 4 tablespoons unsalted butter
- 4 cloves garlic, minced
- 1/4 teaspoon red pepper flakes (optional)
- 1/4 cup dry white wine (such as Pinot Grigio or Sauvignon Blanc)
- Zest and juice of 1 lemon
- 1/4 cup chopped fresh parsley
- Grated Parmesan cheese, for serving
- Lemon wedges, for serving
- Chopped fresh parsley, for garnish (optional)

Instructions:

1. Cook the linguine pasta according to the package instructions in a large pot of salted boiling water until al dente. Reserve 1/2 cup of pasta cooking water, then drain the pasta and set aside.
2. While the pasta is cooking, pat the shrimp dry with paper towels and season them with salt and black pepper to taste.
3. In a large skillet or sauté pan, melt the unsalted butter over medium heat. Add the minced garlic and red pepper flakes (if using) to the skillet and cook for 1-2 minutes until fragrant.
4. Add the seasoned shrimp to the skillet in a single layer. Cook for 2-3 minutes per side, or until the shrimp are pink and opaque.
5. Remove the cooked shrimp from the skillet and set aside.
6. Deglaze the skillet with dry white wine, scraping up any browned bits from the bottom of the pan with a wooden spoon. Let the wine reduce for 1-2 minutes.
7. Stir in the lemon zest and lemon juice, then return the cooked shrimp to the skillet. Add the cooked linguine pasta and chopped fresh parsley to the skillet. Toss everything together until the pasta and shrimp are coated evenly in the sauce.

8. If the sauce seems too dry, add a splash of reserved pasta cooking water to loosen it up.
9. Once everything is heated through, remove the skillet from the heat.
10. Serve the shrimp scampi with linguine hot, garnished with grated Parmesan cheese, lemon wedges, and chopped fresh parsley if desired.
11. Enjoy your delicious shrimp scampi with linguine!

This dish is perfect for a special occasion or a weeknight dinner. It's quick and easy to make, yet it's elegant enough to impress guests. The combination of garlic, lemon, and buttery shrimp is simply irresistible!

Veggie-Packed Turkey Chili

Ingredients:

- 1 tablespoon olive oil
- 1 onion, chopped
- 3 cloves garlic, minced
- 1 lb (450g) ground turkey
- 1 bell pepper, diced
- 1 zucchini, diced
- 1 carrot, diced
- 1 cup corn kernels (fresh, frozen, or canned)
- 1 can (14 oz/400g) diced tomatoes
- 1 can (14 oz/400g) kidney beans, drained and rinsed
- 1 can (14 oz/400g) black beans, drained and rinsed
- 2 cups vegetable broth or chicken broth
- 2 tablespoons chili powder
- 1 teaspoon ground cumin
- 1 teaspoon paprika
- 1/2 teaspoon dried oregano
- Salt and black pepper, to taste
- Optional toppings: shredded cheese, chopped green onions, sour cream, avocado slices, cilantro, etc.

Instructions:

1. Heat olive oil in a large pot or Dutch oven over medium heat. Add the chopped onion and minced garlic to the pot. Cook for 2-3 minutes until softened and fragrant.
2. Add the ground turkey to the pot. Cook, breaking up the meat with a spoon, until browned and cooked through, about 5-7 minutes.
3. Stir in the diced bell pepper, diced zucchini, diced carrot, and corn kernels. Cook for another 5 minutes, or until the vegetables start to soften.
4. Add the diced tomatoes (with their juices), drained and rinsed kidney beans, drained and rinsed black beans, vegetable broth or chicken broth, chili powder, ground cumin, paprika, dried oregano, salt, and black pepper to the pot. Stir to combine.

5. Bring the chili to a simmer, then reduce the heat to low. Cover and let it simmer for 20-25 minutes, stirring occasionally, to allow the flavors to meld together and the vegetables to soften.
6. Once the chili is cooked and the vegetables are tender, taste and adjust the seasoning as needed with salt and black pepper.
7. Serve the veggie-packed turkey chili hot, garnished with your favorite toppings such as shredded cheese, chopped green onions, sour cream, avocado slices, cilantro, etc.
8. Enjoy your hearty and nutritious turkey chili!

This veggie-packed turkey chili is packed with protein, fiber, and vitamins from the turkey and vegetables, making it a healthy and satisfying meal. It's perfect for a chilly day or for meal prep for quick and easy lunches throughout the week.

Lemon Garlic Butter Shrimp and Asparagus

Ingredients:

- 1 lb (450g) large shrimp, peeled and deveined
- Salt and black pepper, to taste
- 2 tablespoons olive oil
- 3 cloves garlic, minced
- 1 bunch asparagus, tough ends trimmed and cut into bite-sized pieces
- Zest and juice of 1 lemon
- 4 tablespoons unsalted butter
- Chopped fresh parsley, for garnish (optional)

Instructions:

1. Season the shrimp with salt and black pepper to taste.
2. Heat olive oil in a large skillet over medium-high heat. Add the minced garlic to the skillet and sauté for 1-2 minutes until fragrant.
3. Add the seasoned shrimp to the skillet in a single layer. Cook for 2-3 minutes per side, or until pink and opaque. Remove the cooked shrimp from the skillet and set aside.
4. In the same skillet, add the bite-sized pieces of asparagus. Sauté for 4-5 minutes, or until tender-crisp.
5. Return the cooked shrimp to the skillet with the asparagus. Add the lemon zest and lemon juice to the skillet.
6. Cut the unsalted butter into tablespoon-sized pieces and add them to the skillet. Stir everything together until the butter is melted and the shrimp and asparagus are coated evenly in the lemon garlic butter sauce.
7. Once everything is heated through and well combined, remove the skillet from the heat.
8. Garnish the lemon garlic butter shrimp and asparagus with chopped fresh parsley, if desired.
9. Serve the dish hot, with rice, pasta, or crusty bread on the side, if desired.
10. Enjoy your delicious and elegant lemon garlic butter shrimp and asparagus!

This dish is perfect for a quick weeknight dinner or for entertaining guests. The combination of tender shrimp, crisp asparagus, and flavorful lemon garlic butter sauce is sure to impress!

Vegetarian Pad Thai

Ingredients:

For the Pad Thai Sauce:

- 1/4 cup soy sauce
- 2 tablespoons tamarind paste (or substitute with lime juice)
- 2 tablespoons brown sugar (or palm sugar)
- 1 tablespoon rice vinegar
- 1 tablespoon Sriracha sauce (adjust to taste)
- 2 cloves garlic, minced
- 1 teaspoon grated ginger
- 1 tablespoon vegetable oil

For the Pad Thai:

- 8 oz (225g) rice noodles
- 2 tablespoons vegetable oil
- 2 eggs, lightly beaten (optional, omit for vegan version)
- 1 cup firm tofu, diced
- 1 cup mixed vegetables (such as bell peppers, carrots, broccoli, bean sprouts)
- 4 green onions, chopped
- 1/4 cup chopped peanuts (optional, for garnish)
- Fresh cilantro leaves, for garnish (optional)
- Lime wedges, for serving

Instructions:

1. In a small bowl, whisk together all the ingredients for the Pad Thai sauce: soy sauce, tamarind paste (or lime juice), brown sugar, rice vinegar, Sriracha sauce, minced garlic, grated ginger, and vegetable oil. Set aside.
2. Cook the rice noodles according to the package instructions until al dente. Drain and rinse under cold water to stop the cooking process. Set aside.

3. In a large skillet or wok, heat 1 tablespoon of vegetable oil over medium-high heat. If using eggs, pour them into the skillet and scramble until cooked. Remove the cooked eggs from the skillet and set aside.
4. In the same skillet, add another tablespoon of vegetable oil. Add the diced tofu to the skillet and cook until lightly browned on all sides, about 5-7 minutes. Remove the tofu from the skillet and set aside.
5. Add the mixed vegetables to the skillet and stir-fry for 3-4 minutes, or until tender-crisp.
6. Add the cooked rice noodles, scrambled eggs (if using), cooked tofu, and chopped green onions to the skillet. Pour the Pad Thai sauce over the ingredients in the skillet.
7. Using tongs or chopsticks, toss everything together until well combined and heated through.
8. Once everything is heated through and well coated in the sauce, remove the skillet from the heat.
9. Serve the vegetarian Pad Thai hot, garnished with chopped peanuts (if using), fresh cilantro leaves, and lime wedges on the side.
10. Enjoy your delicious vegetarian Pad Thai!

This dish is customizable, so feel free to add your favorite vegetables or protein options.

It's a satisfying and flavorful meal that's perfect for a quick and easy dinner.

Creamy Mushroom Spinach Tortellini Soup

Ingredients:

- 1 tablespoon olive oil
- 1 onion, diced
- 3 cloves garlic, minced
- 8 oz (225g) mushrooms, sliced
- 4 cups vegetable broth or chicken broth
- 1 teaspoon dried thyme
- 1 teaspoon dried oregano
- 1/2 teaspoon dried basil
- Salt and black pepper, to taste
- 9 oz (255g) fresh or frozen cheese tortellini
- 2 cups fresh spinach leaves
- 1 cup heavy cream or half-and-half
- Grated Parmesan cheese, for serving (optional)
- Chopped fresh parsley, for garnish (optional)

Instructions:

1. In a large pot or Dutch oven, heat olive oil over medium heat. Add the diced onion and minced garlic to the pot. Cook for 2-3 minutes until softened and fragrant.
2. Add the sliced mushrooms to the pot. Cook for 5-6 minutes, or until the mushrooms are softened and golden brown.
3. Pour the vegetable broth or chicken broth into the pot. Add the dried thyme, dried oregano, dried basil, salt, and black pepper to taste. Stir to combine.
4. Bring the soup to a simmer. Once simmering, add the cheese tortellini to the pot. Cook according to the package instructions until the tortellini are tender.
5. Stir in the fresh spinach leaves and cook for 1-2 minutes until wilted.
6. Reduce the heat to low and stir in the heavy cream or half-and-half. Heat the soup gently for another 2-3 minutes, making sure not to let it boil.
7. Once heated through, taste the soup and adjust the seasoning with salt and black pepper if needed.
8. Ladle the creamy mushroom spinach tortellini soup into bowls. Garnish with grated Parmesan cheese and chopped fresh parsley, if desired.
9. Serve the soup hot, with crusty bread or garlic bread on the side, if desired.
10. Enjoy your comforting and delicious creamy mushroom spinach tortellini soup!

This soup is rich, creamy, and packed with flavor from the mushrooms, spinach, and cheese tortellini. It's sure to warm you up on a chilly day and is perfect for a comforting meal any time of the year.

Sheet Pan Garlic Herb Pork Chops with Potatoes

Ingredients:

For the Garlic Herb Marinade:

- 4 cloves garlic, minced
- 2 tablespoons olive oil
- 1 tablespoon chopped fresh rosemary
- 1 tablespoon chopped fresh thyme
- 1 tablespoon chopped fresh parsley
- 1 teaspoon Dijon mustard
- Salt and black pepper, to taste

For the Pork Chops and Potatoes:

- 4 bone-in pork chops, about 1-inch thick
- 1 lb (450g) baby potatoes, halved or quartered if large
- 2 tablespoons olive oil
- Salt and black pepper, to taste
- Additional chopped fresh herbs for garnish (optional)

Instructions:

1. Preheat your oven to 400°F (200°C). Line a large baking sheet with parchment paper or aluminum foil for easy cleanup.
2. In a small bowl, whisk together the minced garlic, olive oil, chopped fresh rosemary, thyme, parsley, Dijon mustard, salt, and black pepper to make the garlic herb marinade.
3. Pat the pork chops dry with paper towels. Place them in a shallow dish or resealable plastic bag. Pour the garlic herb marinade over the pork chops, making sure they are evenly coated. Allow them to marinate for at least 30 minutes, or refrigerate for up to 4 hours for best flavor.
4. In a large bowl, toss the halved baby potatoes with olive oil, salt, and black pepper until evenly coated.

5. Arrange the marinated pork chops and seasoned potatoes on the prepared baking sheet in a single layer, leaving space between them.
6. Roast in the preheated oven for 20-25 minutes, or until the pork chops reach an internal temperature of 145°F (63°C) and the potatoes are tender and golden brown, flipping the pork chops and stirring the potatoes halfway through cooking.
7. Once done, remove the sheet pan from the oven and let the pork chops rest for a few minutes before serving.
8. Garnish with additional chopped fresh herbs, if desired, and serve hot.
9. Enjoy your delicious sheet pan garlic herb pork chops with potatoes!

This dish is simple to prepare and packed with flavor from the garlic herb marinade. The pork chops are juicy and tender, while the roasted potatoes are crispy on the outside and fluffy on the inside. It's a satisfying meal that the whole family will love!

Baked Honey Mustard Chicken with Brussels Sprouts

Ingredients:

For the Honey Mustard Marinade:

- 1/4 cup Dijon mustard
- 2 tablespoons honey
- 2 tablespoons olive oil
- 2 cloves garlic, minced
- 1 tablespoon apple cider vinegar
- 1 teaspoon dried thyme
- Salt and black pepper, to taste

For the Chicken and Brussels Sprouts:

- 4 boneless, skinless chicken breasts
- 1 lb (450g) Brussels sprouts, trimmed and halved
- 2 tablespoons olive oil
- Salt and black pepper, to taste
- Chopped fresh parsley, for garnish (optional)

Instructions:

1. Preheat your oven to 400°F (200°C). Line a large baking sheet with parchment paper or aluminum foil for easy cleanup.
2. In a small bowl, whisk together the Dijon mustard, honey, olive oil, minced garlic, apple cider vinegar, dried thyme, salt, and black pepper to make the honey mustard marinade.
3. Place the chicken breasts in a shallow dish or resealable plastic bag. Pour half of the honey mustard marinade over the chicken breasts, making sure they are evenly coated. Reserve the remaining marinade for later.
4. In a separate bowl, toss the halved Brussels sprouts with olive oil, salt, and black pepper until evenly coated.
5. Arrange the marinated chicken breasts and seasoned Brussels sprouts on the prepared baking sheet in a single layer, leaving space between them.

6. Bake in the preheated oven for 20-25 minutes, or until the chicken is cooked through (reaching an internal temperature of 165°F/75°C) and the Brussels sprouts are tender and caramelized, flipping the chicken halfway through cooking.
7. Once done, remove the baking sheet from the oven and brush the cooked chicken breasts with the reserved honey mustard marinade.
8. Garnish with chopped fresh parsley, if desired, and serve hot.
9. Enjoy your delicious baked honey mustard chicken with Brussels sprouts!

This dish is a wonderful combination of sweet and tangy flavors from the honey mustard marinade, paired with the earthy taste of roasted Brussels sprouts. It's a wholesome and satisfying meal that's sure to become a family favorite!

Coconut Curry Shrimp with Rice

Ingredients:

For the Coconut Curry Sauce:

- 1 tablespoon vegetable oil
- 1 onion, finely chopped
- 3 cloves garlic, minced
- 1 tablespoon grated ginger
- 2 tablespoons red curry paste
- 1 can (13.5 oz/400ml) coconut milk
- 1 tablespoon soy sauce
- 1 tablespoon brown sugar
- Juice of 1 lime
- Salt and pepper to taste

For the Shrimp:

- 1 lb (450g) large shrimp, peeled and deveined
- 2 tablespoons vegetable oil
- Salt and pepper to taste
- Chopped fresh cilantro, for garnish (optional)
- Cooked rice, for serving

Instructions:

1. Heat 1 tablespoon of vegetable oil in a large skillet or wok over medium heat. Add the chopped onion and cook until softened, about 3-4 minutes.
2. Add the minced garlic and grated ginger to the skillet, and cook for another 1-2 minutes until fragrant.
3. Stir in the red curry paste and cook for 1 minute, stirring constantly to release its flavors.
4. Pour in the coconut milk, soy sauce, brown sugar, and lime juice. Stir to combine and bring the mixture to a simmer. Let it simmer for 5-7 minutes to allow the

flavors to meld together and the sauce to thicken slightly. Season with salt and pepper to taste.
5. While the sauce is simmering, prepare the shrimp. Pat the shrimp dry with paper towels and season with salt and pepper.
6. In a separate skillet, heat 2 tablespoons of vegetable oil over medium-high heat. Add the seasoned shrimp to the skillet in a single layer and cook for 2-3 minutes per side, or until pink and opaque.
7. Once the shrimp are cooked, transfer them to the simmering coconut curry sauce. Stir to coat the shrimp in the sauce.
8. Serve the coconut curry shrimp hot, over cooked rice. Garnish with chopped fresh cilantro, if desired.
9. Enjoy your delicious coconut curry shrimp with rice!

This dish is creamy, fragrant, and packed with flavor from the coconut milk and red curry paste. It's perfect for a quick and satisfying weeknight dinner or for entertaining guests.

Veggie Quesadillas with Guacamole

Ingredients:

For the Veggie Quesadillas:

- 4 large flour tortillas
- 1 cup shredded cheese (such as cheddar, Monterey Jack, or a Mexican blend)
- 1 bell pepper, thinly sliced
- 1 onion, thinly sliced
- 1 cup sliced mushrooms
- 1 cup cooked black beans (canned is fine)
- 1 teaspoon ground cumin
- 1 teaspoon chili powder
- Salt and pepper to taste
- Olive oil or cooking spray

For the Guacamole:

- 2 ripe avocados
- 1 tomato, diced
- 1/4 cup finely chopped red onion
- 1/4 cup chopped fresh cilantro
- Juice of 1 lime
- Salt and pepper to taste

Instructions:

1. Preheat a large skillet or griddle over medium heat.
2. In a small bowl, mash the avocados to your desired consistency for the guacamole. Stir in the diced tomato, chopped red onion, chopped cilantro, lime juice, salt, and pepper. Mix well and set aside.
3. In the same skillet or griddle, heat a small amount of olive oil or cooking spray over medium heat. Place one flour tortilla in the skillet.

4. Sprinkle a layer of shredded cheese evenly over half of the tortilla. Top the cheese with a layer of sliced bell pepper, sliced onion, sliced mushrooms, and cooked black beans. Sprinkle the vegetables with ground cumin, chili powder, salt, and pepper to taste.
5. Fold the other half of the tortilla over the filling to create a half-moon shape. Press down gently with a spatula to seal the quesadilla.
6. Cook the quesadilla for 2-3 minutes on each side, or until golden brown and crispy, and the cheese is melted. Repeat with the remaining tortillas and filling ingredients.
7. Once cooked, remove the quesadillas from the skillet and let them cool for a minute or two before slicing them into wedges.
8. Serve the veggie quesadillas hot, with a side of guacamole for dipping.
9. Enjoy your delicious veggie quesadillas with guacamole!

These veggie quesadillas are packed with flavor from the colorful vegetables and melted cheese, while the guacamole adds a creamy and tangy element to the dish.

They're perfect for a quick and satisfying meal any time of the day!

One-Pot Lemon Herb Chicken and Rice

Ingredients:

- 4 bone-in, skin-on chicken thighs (or any chicken pieces of your choice)
- Salt and pepper, to taste
- 2 tablespoons olive oil
- 1 onion, finely chopped
- 3 cloves garlic, minced
- 1 cup long-grain white rice
- 2 cups chicken broth
- Zest and juice of 1 lemon
- 1 teaspoon dried thyme
- 1 teaspoon dried rosemary
- 1/2 teaspoon dried oregano
- 1/2 teaspoon paprika
- 1/4 teaspoon red pepper flakes (optional)
- Fresh parsley, chopped, for garnish (optional)
- Lemon wedges, for serving

Instructions:

1. Season the chicken thighs with salt and pepper on both sides.
2. Heat olive oil in a large skillet or Dutch oven over medium-high heat. Add the chicken thighs, skin-side down, and cook until golden brown, about 5 minutes. Flip and cook for an additional 5 minutes. Remove the chicken from the skillet and set aside.
3. In the same skillet, add the chopped onion and cook until softened, about 3-4 minutes. Add the minced garlic and cook for another 1 minute until fragrant.
4. Add the rice to the skillet and stir to coat it in the oil, onion, and garlic mixture.
5. Pour in the chicken broth, lemon zest, lemon juice, dried thyme, dried rosemary, dried oregano, paprika, and red pepper flakes (if using). Stir to combine.
6. Return the browned chicken thighs to the skillet, nestling them into the rice mixture.
7. Bring the mixture to a simmer, then reduce the heat to low. Cover and let it cook for 20-25 minutes, or until the rice is tender and the chicken is cooked through, with an internal temperature of 165°F (75°C).

8. Once done, remove the skillet from the heat and let it sit, covered, for 5 minutes.
9. Garnish with chopped fresh parsley, if desired, and serve hot with lemon wedges on the side.
10. Enjoy your delicious one-pot lemon herb chicken and rice!

This dish is bursting with flavor from the lemon and herbs, and the chicken thighs remain tender and juicy as they cook alongside the rice. It's a comforting and wholesome meal that the whole family will love!

Black Bean and Corn Stuffed Sweet Potatoes

Ingredients:

- 4 medium sweet potatoes
- 1 tablespoon olive oil
- 1 small onion, diced
- 2 cloves garlic, minced
- 1 bell pepper, diced (any color)
- 1 cup canned black beans, drained and rinsed
- 1 cup frozen corn kernels, thawed
- 1 teaspoon ground cumin
- 1/2 teaspoon chili powder
- Salt and pepper, to taste
- 1/4 cup chopped fresh cilantro
- 1 avocado, sliced (for garnish)
- Lime wedges, for serving

Instructions:

1. Preheat your oven to 400°F (200°C). Line a baking sheet with parchment paper.
2. Scrub the sweet potatoes and pierce each one several times with a fork. Place them on the prepared baking sheet and bake for 45-60 minutes, or until tender when pierced with a fork.
3. While the sweet potatoes are baking, heat olive oil in a large skillet over medium heat. Add the diced onion and bell pepper to the skillet and cook until softened, about 5 minutes.
4. Add the minced garlic to the skillet and cook for another 1-2 minutes until fragrant.
5. Stir in the black beans, corn kernels, ground cumin, chili powder, salt, and pepper. Cook for 3-4 minutes, stirring occasionally, until heated through.
6. Once the sweet potatoes are done baking, carefully slice each one open lengthwise and fluff the flesh with a fork.
7. Spoon the black bean and corn mixture into each sweet potato, dividing it evenly among them.
8. Garnish the stuffed sweet potatoes with chopped fresh cilantro and sliced avocado.

9. Serve hot, with lime wedges on the side for squeezing over the top.
10. Enjoy your delicious black bean and corn stuffed sweet potatoes!

These stuffed sweet potatoes are packed with flavor and texture from the black beans, corn, and aromatic spices. They make for a satisfying and wholesome meal that's perfect for lunch or dinner.

Creamy Tomato Basil Soup with Grilled Cheese

Ingredients:

- 2 tablespoons olive oil
- 1 onion, chopped
- 2 cloves garlic, minced
- 2 cans (28 oz each) whole peeled tomatoes
- 1 cup vegetable broth
- 1/2 cup heavy cream
- 1/4 cup chopped fresh basil leaves
- Salt and pepper, to taste
- Pinch of sugar (optional, to balance acidity)

Instructions:

1. Heat olive oil in a large pot over medium heat. Add chopped onion and cook until softened, about 5 minutes.
2. Add minced garlic and cook for another 1-2 minutes until fragrant.
3. Add the canned tomatoes (with their juices) to the pot. Use a spoon to break up the tomatoes into smaller pieces.
4. Pour in the vegetable broth and bring the mixture to a simmer. Let it simmer for about 15-20 minutes, stirring occasionally.
5. Using an immersion blender or regular blender, puree the soup until smooth. Return it to the pot if using a regular blender.
6. Stir in the heavy cream and chopped fresh basil. Season with salt, pepper, and a pinch of sugar to taste.
7. Let the soup simmer for another 5-10 minutes to allow the flavors to meld together.
8. Serve hot, garnished with additional fresh basil leaves if desired.

Grilled Cheese:

Ingredients:

- 8 slices of bread
- Butter, softened
- 8 slices of your favorite cheese (such as cheddar, Swiss, or American)

Instructions:

1. Heat a large skillet or griddle over medium heat.
2. Butter one side of each slice of bread.
3. Place 4 slices of bread, butter-side down, on the skillet or griddle.
4. Top each slice of bread with a slice of cheese, then cover with another slice of bread, butter-side up.
5. Cook the sandwiches for 2-3 minutes on each side, or until golden brown and the cheese is melted.
6. Remove the grilled cheese sandwiches from the skillet or griddle and let them cool for a minute before slicing.
7. Serve hot, alongside the creamy tomato basil soup.
8. Enjoy your delicious creamy tomato basil soup with grilled cheese sandwiches!

This classic combination is sure to warm you up on a chilly day and is perfect for a comforting meal anytime.

Szechuan Tofu and Green Beans Stir-Fry

Ingredients:

- 14 oz (400g) firm tofu, drained and cut into cubes
- 1 lb (450g) green beans, trimmed and cut into bite-sized pieces
- 2 tablespoons vegetable oil
- 3 cloves garlic, minced
- 1 tablespoon grated ginger
- 2 tablespoons soy sauce
- 1 tablespoon hoisin sauce
- 1 tablespoon rice vinegar
- 1 tablespoon chili garlic sauce (adjust to taste)
- 1 teaspoon sesame oil
- 1 teaspoon cornstarch mixed with 2 tablespoons water
- Sesame seeds, for garnish (optional)
- Sliced green onions, for garnish (optional)
- Cooked rice, for serving

Instructions:

1. Heat vegetable oil in a large skillet or wok over medium-high heat.
2. Add the tofu cubes to the skillet in a single layer. Cook for 3-4 minutes per side, or until golden brown and crispy. Remove the tofu from the skillet and set aside.
3. In the same skillet, add a bit more oil if needed. Add minced garlic and grated ginger to the skillet and cook for 1-2 minutes until fragrant.
4. Add the green beans to the skillet and stir-fry for 5-6 minutes, or until crisp-tender.
5. In a small bowl, whisk together soy sauce, hoisin sauce, rice vinegar, chili garlic sauce, and sesame oil.
6. Return the cooked tofu to the skillet with the green beans. Pour the sauce over the tofu and green beans, stirring to coat evenly.
7. Stir in the cornstarch mixture and cook for another 1-2 minutes until the sauce has thickened.
8. Remove the skillet from the heat and garnish with sesame seeds and sliced green onions, if desired.
9. Serve hot, over cooked rice.

10. Enjoy your delicious Szechuan tofu and green beans stir-fry!

This dish is full of bold flavors from the Szechuan sauce, and the combination of tofu and green beans makes it a satisfying and nutritious meal. It's perfect for a quick and flavorful dinner any day of the week!